Few people have impacted God's king He is one of the most anointed and transformative voices in Christendom, and his latest book, *The Finale*, serves as both a prophetic and practical prescription for this time of unprecedented change. Without a doubt Pastor Parsley's latest contribution will inform, inspire, and impart grace, truth, and faith as we await the return of Jesus Christ.

—Rev. Samuel Rodriguez
President, National Hispanic Christian Leadership
Conference
Hispanic Evangelical Association

One of the most important things about Rod Parsley's new book, *The Finale*, is the second chapter, "Untangling the Timeline." So many people struggle with the Book of Revelation and the end times, but there is no need to. One of the keys is the timeline. Anything from the heart and pen of Rod Parsley is a must-read.

—Kenneth Copeland
Kenneth Copeland Ministries

The death and resurrection of Jesus Christ are already matters of historical record. The next event on God's cosmic calendar is His return, of course. And who better to explain its immediacy and primacy than Rod Parsley?

—Mike Huckabee
New York Times Best-Selling Author
Former Governor, Former Television and Radio Host

Pastor Rod Parsley's books are such easy and delightful reads, and this third book in his trilogy about Jesus is no exception. *The Finale* begins with fascinating history that sets the stage for the final great events that accompany the return of Jesus Christ to the earth after His ascension to heaven. Parsley establishes a timeline based on certain specifics the scriptures mention that will hopefully cause us to do more thinking about end-time events than fighting over how and when they will occur. Read, enjoy, get prepared—it will soon unfold.

—MARCUS D. LAMB
FOUNDER AND PRESIDENT, DAYSTAR TELEVISION NETWORK

Jesus Christ, our beginning and the end! As we have traveled with Dr. Rod Parsley along this journey, in his conclusion book of his trilogy, *The Finale: One World...One Ruler...One Reign...*, we come to a revealed climax that is certain to propel you forward to an astounding revelation of Jesus Christ. Moving from such rigidly religious intentions, this is a must-read primer for those gasping for a breath of millennial understanding. Encapsulating the saints' expected end through our glorious hope's return, Jesus Christ!

—MEDINA PULLINGS
MEDINA PULLINGS MINISTRIES
COPASTOR, UNITED NATIONS CHURCH INTERNATIONAL

Pastor Rod Parsley once again delves into his deep reservoir of biblical understanding to produce this much-needed eschatological masterpiece! It's a must-read for every serious student of the Bible, as well as for every believer who desires a greater understanding of the prophecies and symbols of the Book of Revelation and end-time events!

—PASTOR DARRELL SCOTT
NEW SPIRIT REVIVAL CENTER

In *The Finale* my dear friend Rod Parsley does a masterful job of outlining and explaining the events leading to the return of our Lord Jesus Christ. It's profound enough for the most studious scholar, yet simple enough for the new believer. Best of all it is a no-nonsense, straight-ahead approach to eschatology. This is a much-needed and long-anticipated book that should be read by everyone who is looking forward to our Lord's glorious, soon-coming return!

—Pastor Benny Hinn
Benny Hinn Ministries

In *The Finale*, a worthy successor to his previous works, *The Cross* and *Gone*, Rod Parsley captures the essence of eschatology. With refreshing insight and clear-headed reasoning, Parsley explains the events of the end times in terms everyone can understand. Christ is the victor, the plan of God rules supreme, and we, the believers, are the beneficiaries.

—Bishop George Bloomer
Bethel Family Worship Center

T H E

THE

FINALE

ROD **PARSLEY**

CHARISMA
HOUSE

Most CHARISMA HOUSE BOOK GROUP products are available at special quantity discounts for bulk purchase for sales promotions, premiums, fund-raising, and educational needs. For details, write Charisma House Book Group, 600 Rinehart Road, Lake Mary, Florida 32746, or telephone (407) 333-0600.

THE FINALE by Rod Parsley
Published by Charisma House
Charisma Media/Charisma House Book Group
600 Rinehart Road
Lake Mary, Florida 32746
www.charismahouse.com

Cover design by Cameron Fontana
Design director: Justin Evans

Visit the author's website at www.rodparsley.com.

Library of Congress Cataloging-in-Publication Data:
Names: Parsley, Rod, author.
Title: The finale / Rod Parsley.
Description: Lake Mary, Florida : Charisma House, 2017. | Includes bibliographical references.
Identifiers: LCCN 2016059468| ISBN 9781629991733 (trade paper) | ISBN 9781629991740 (ebook)
Subjects: LCSH: Second Advent. | Second Advent--Biblical teaching.
Classification: LCC BT886.3 .P37 2017 | DDC 236/.9--dc23
LC record available at https://lccn.loc.gov/2016059468

17 18 19 20 21 — 9 8 7 6 5 4 3 2
Printed in the United States of America

Contents

Foreword

IN THE EPIC conclusion to his trilogy detailing the three most significant events in the history of the world, Pastor Rod Parsley presents *The Finale: One World... One Ruler... One Reign....*

The biblical promise of the return of Christ is and has been widely accepted throughout Christianity, but many believers harbor fear rather than hope regarding latter-day prophecy. *The Finale* helps one trade fear for faith, replaces concern with comfort and confidence, as Pastor Parsley passionately examines the truth of God's Word about Christ's return.

Understanding Bible prophecy can, and must, affect the way we live. In Pastor Parsley's own words, "This is a road map for living victoriously and fruitfully in the volatile days leading up to our glorious departure. It is a guide for experiencing peace in the midst of our raging cultural storms." This is not simply a book of facts but a reflection of his personal, prayer-filled study of the Word and end-time events and what it means for each of us today.

—DR. JACK VAN IMPE
JACK VAN IMPE MINISTRIES INTERNATIONAL

Prologue

*Make haste, my beloved, and be like a gazelle or a
young stag on the mountains of spices!*

—SONG OF SONGS 8:14

Cana, Galilee, 4 BC

FOR WHAT MAY be the twenty-third time this day, Avigail moves to the tiny window of her father's house and intently scans the horizon. Her deep brown almond-shaped eyes squint against a reddening sun now lowering itself onto the fertile, rolling Galilean hills. The earthy scents of freshly cut grain and livestock waft through the opening as she seeks any sign of movement in the distance—perhaps a telltale cloud of rising dust from the road just beyond a distant knoll—anything that might indicate the approach of an entourage.

Nothing stirs, save a pair of eagles soaring effortlessly on the late afternoon thermals.

Avigail sighs, glances at the silver betrothal ring on her finger, and returns to the table where she has been filling a series of small earthenware lamps with oil for the night. She will keep one burning in the window through the dark hours.

It's been almost a year since her betrothed went away. In accordance with ancient Jewish custom, he departed immediately following their engagement ceremony feast to prepare their new home. She knows the day of his return for her must surely be imminent. When her beloved arrives—whether at noon or even at midnight—she will be ready. At eighteen years of age, it is time for Avigail to be married. Yet the customs and traditions that prescribe how such a union should be arranged, prepared for, and consummated are as specific as they are ancient.

When she was sixteen, Avigail's father informed her that a suitable husband had been identified and that her *mohar*, the bride price, had been successfully negotiated with the father of the prospective groom. Everyone involved agreed it was an excellent match. The groom's father hailed from a wealthy and successful Jerusalem family. Avigail's father was of more modest means but well respected for his moral excellence and zeal for the law of Moses. It was also no secret that this adolescent daughter was strikingly beautiful and renowned for her grace and charm. Even so, whispers of the extravagantly high *mohar* Avigail had commanded from this aristocratic family flew through the tightly knit communities sprinkled across the hills west of the Sea of Galilee. *Such a price!*

The intricate courtship ritual of the *shiddukhin*, the Jewish matchmaking process, had begun with some written correspondence followed by a personal visit by a well-dressed emissary, or agent, from Jerusalem representing the groom's father. Many were surprised to see a prominent Jerusalem family expressing interest in a girl from rural Galilee, even if she was the daughter of one of Cana's most respected landowners. Jewish residents of busy, cosmopolitan Jerusalem often looked down their noses at their country cousins to the north, who were identified by their distinctive accent. But Avigail's father had many relatives in Judea and visited Jerusalem frequently for both worship and business. He was not unknown there.

A year of exciting milestones followed in quick succession, all in accordance with the ancient time-honored traditions of the Israelite tribes.

Early in the process came the day the young people met for

the first time. It was a tense occasion for all involved—not least for the two at the center of this delicate business. Even in a patriarchal culture Jewish custom clearly stated that the young man's preferences had to be considered. If Avigail did not please him, he had the right to ask his father to stop the process.

Far more surprising, given the age and religious culture, was that Avigail too had a say in the matter. The sacred customs of her people clearly stated that the prospective bride also had to approve of the match. Yes, the bridegroom must set his affections upon the bride, but if a marriage was to be arranged and consummated, she had to choose as well.

Fortunately both sides in this love equation were instantly enamored. He was smitten at their first introduction. She felt much the same, finding this young man more than sufficiently handsome and wealthy. As important to her, he was clearly kind, thoughtful, and virtuous.

This auspicious beginning led directly to settling the amount of the *mohar* to be paid by the groom's father. In the months that followed, a steady stream of additional gifts from the bridegroom found their way to Avigail's doorstep. Such gifts, called *mattan*, or love gifts, were not strictly required by custom, but they were common when the bridegroom wanted to show his commitment and devotion to his future bride. Given both the frequency and the quality of the *mattan* Avigail's intended showered upon her in this initial phase of this lengthy process, the young bridegroom was clearly both wealthy and very much in love.

The next major milestone on the Jewish courtship calendar was the betrothal ceremony—the *kiddushin*. This was not the wedding ceremony, but it was no less binding. A betrothed couple was married for all legal purposes, even though physical union and cohabitation were at least a year away. A betrothal was unbreakable and irrevocable, except by death or infidelity.

Two critical events lay at the heart of the *kiddushin*.

One was the signing of the agreement between the two

respective fathers of the couple. This contract spelled out the agreed-upon amount of the "bride price," the size of her dowry, as well as any other stipulations agreed upon by both parties.

However, before the fathers' signatures or seals put this sacred, binding contract into force, one last symbolic step was often taken—the pouring and drinking of the cup of acceptance. Avigail's future bridegroom poured a cup of wine, spoke a blessing over it, and presented it to his future bride. The room fell utterly silent, and every eye focused on her. To drink would be to signify she was willing to enter into this lifetime bond.

Avigail accepted and drank from the cup. The act was met with a roar of delight from the assembled families. Their covenant of commitment and love was sealed. The couple were officially betrothed.

The engagement period typically lasted one full year. This season of waiting served two practical purposes. First, it allowed the groom to return to his father's lands and build a dwelling place for the newlyweds. Often this was a multi-room addition to the father's house. The second function was no less necessary. A waiting period of more than nine months assured everyone involved that the prospective bride was not already with child. Turning up pregnant in the middle of the betrothal year was a scandalous problem with immense implications. Indeed, just such a scandal would soon unfold a few miles south of Cana, in the nearby village of Nazareth, involving a young girl named Mary.

The bride was left to anticipate the return of the groom. Although she would know the general season in which to expect his arrival, the precise time was a mystery to her. In fact, the groom did not know either. His father alone determined that the preparations on the bridegroom's end were complete and that the time for bringing his bride home had finally arrived. It is easy to understand why wise tradition did not leave this decision in the hands of the bridegroom. A healthy young man eager to get to the wedding night bed-chamber and take his beloved into his arms could easily be prone to rushing the preparations.

No, the calmer, more dispassionate judgment of the father rather than that of the lovesick son set the precise timing of his return for his bride. When the father gave the signal, the ecstatic bridegroom and an entourage of friends were dispatched to, in a sense, *abduct* the bride. This *nissuin*, as it is called, literally means "the taking," and it lies at the root of the Jewish saying to "take a wife." These sudden snatchings away, announced only by a blast from a shofar and a shout, often occurred at midnight. Thus a prudent, expectant bride kept one or two oil lamps filled and ready at all times.

The bride also used this yearlong period of waiting to prepare her wedding garments. Her wedding day raiment would be spotless white—unsoiled by the defiling grime of the wider world—and intricately detailed. Avigail had done so. The fully prepared bride then entered the anxious season of waiting and watching.

Permit me a personal aside here. Thirty years of walking through life together as husband and wife have taught my amazing bride, Joni, and me a few things about patience and even a little about the end times.

We dated for seven years as I was busy with a rapidly expanding ministry. Some amused onlookers among our friends and family refer to this seemingly endless span as the "Tribulation Period." Sweet, long-suffering Joni. When I finally gave her an engagement ring, I had the nerve to ask her not to wear it until I had the opportunity to discuss our wedding date with my mentor, Dr. Lester Sumrall! Can you imagine asking a girl who has waited seven long years for that ring to hold it yet not wear it? The woman deserves a medal.

Eventually we were married, and our wedding night was like the "Rapture." Two beautiful children eventually came along, but getting them to adulthood has at times seemed like the "Millennium."

In all seriousness the Word of God consistently points to the betrothal and marriage of a man and woman in purity as an earthly echo of a profound and powerful heavenly truth concerning the Lord Jesus Christ and His relentless, tenacious love for you and me. Paul called this "a great mystery."[1]

As we're about to see, those same holy Scriptures deploy the exquisitely beautiful imagery of betrothal and marriage to bring us light and understanding of His plans to bring history to a predetermined close of His sovereign choosing. In other words, the holy consummation of a marriage parallels the completion of God's grand redemptive plan of the ages.

The one-year anniversary of Avigail's betrothal has come and gone. "Why hasn't he returned for me yet?" she wonders. "Why the delay? Perhaps he has been in an accident? Maybe he's had a change of heart. What if he has met someone he finds more attractive?" She silences her inner voice of fear and doubt by noting the numerous *mattan* love gifts that now fill her trousseau. Each gift represents a pledge or guarantee of his love.

Avigail attempts to distract herself by throwing herself into household chores. Yet the any-moment arrival of her betrothed is never far from her mind.

A sudden sound from outside causes her to rush to the window. "Is that a shofar sounding?" She hushes the other members of the household as she listens intently. It is only the protest of a braying donkey at a neighboring farm. She breathes another heavy sigh and returns to her work beside her mother.

He promised to return for her. So she waits. She watches. She listens.

The bridegroom will come. He promised he would, and she believes him. When he does, he will find her ready.

CHAPTER 1

The Promise

The primitive church thought more about the Second Coming of Jesus Christ than about death or about heaven. The early Christians were looking not for a cleft in the ground called a grave but for a cleavage in the sky called Glory. They were watching not for the undertaker but for the uppertaker.[1]

—ALEXANDER MACLAREN (1826–1910)

ELEVEN MEN STAND on a Judean hilltop staring slack-jawed, silent, and still at a cloud in the sky above them. Moments before, just outside Jerusalem on a summit called Olivet, they had watched their leader and friend exit Planet Earth. They had seen Him accomplish many other astonishing things during the time they had known Him, but this was both unprecedented and utterly unexpected.

One moment they were speaking with Him just as they had done so often during the previous forty days since His horrifying death and miraculous, third-day resurrection. The next moment He was loosened from the law of gravity and rising skyward above the realm of men, becoming smaller and smaller until He was eclipsed altogether by the billowing clouds.

No one spoke. No one moved. Eleven pairs of eyes simply blinked and stared at the sky in a whirlwind of befuddlement and awe. Without warning, a mighty voice from behind them startled them nearly out of their skins. The disciples wheeled around to see two giant men dressed in dazzling white, one of whom was addressing them:

> Men of Galilee, why stand looking toward heaven? This
> same Jesus, who was taken up from you to heaven, will
> come in like manner as you saw Him go into heaven.
>   —ACTS 1:11

Thus the same eleven who were among the first to recognize that the promised Savior had come to earth also became the very first to receive a new heavenly promise.

He will return.

Yes, allow me without fear of contradiction to state it as Kentucky plain as I can: Jesus, Jehovah Joshua Messiah—the Lord Jesus Christ—is coming back to earth.

Across the diverse spectrum of global Christianity there is almost universal agreement on this point. Catholics, Protestants, mainline denominations, evangelicals, synods, societies, and sects of every stripe affirm this truth without hesitation. They always have. The most ancient creeds of the church codified this expectation directly into the confessions that defined Christian orthodoxy. For example, in the early fourth century the Nicene Creed declared that Jesus had "ascended into the heavens" and "shall come to judge the quick and the dead." [2]

Throughout the gospel's relentless and glorious march through history, the great leaders of the Christian church have affirmed, declared, and decreed the certainty of that angelic Mount of Olives promise. One of the oldest nonbiblical writings, the *Didache*, believed to have been written in the late first century—when many of the apostles were still living—exhorts the faithful to be ready at any moment:

> Watch over your life; your lamps must not go out, nor
> your loins be ungirded; on the contrary, be ready. You do
> not know the hour in which Our Lord is coming. [3]

In the third century the early church father Cyprian of Carthage wrote: "Antichrist cometh, but upon him cometh also Christ."[4] Twelve centuries later the reformer Martin Luther closed a benediction with the words, "Come, dear Lord Jesus! And whoever loves You, let him say, 'Come, dear Lord Jesus.'"[5]

In that same era eschatology fueled the efforts of Christopher Columbus to find a shorter, westward route to Asia. The explorer knew well Jesus's words in Matthew 24:14, a passage filled with end-time significance: "And this gospel of the kingdom will be preached throughout the world as a testimony to all nations, and then the end will come." One historian described Columbus's reasoning and motives this way:

> [He] held a millennialist faith derived from an assiduous study of scripture and from a familiarity with the eschatology of Joachim of Fiore.... If there were a shortcut to the East by sea, missionaries could be sent there faster and Christians could meet the provision for world evangelization before the Lord could return.... Like John the Baptist at the first coming, he [would help] prepare the way for the second.[6]

The expectation that Jesus would return to this blue marble planet traveled across the Atlantic with the first American colonists. Jonathan Edwards (1703–1758), a spiritual father of the Great Awakening and a preacher of incalculable influence, certainly held this view. In a sermon titled "The Final Judgment" the Puritan preacher reminded his congregation:

> The person by whom God will judge the world is Jesus Christ, God-man. The second person in the Trinity...will come to judge the world both in his divine and human nature, in the same human body that was crucified, and rose again, and ascended up into heaven.[7]

I wish today that the pulpits of this wandering and wondering world, beginning in America, would thunder once again these timeless truths!

Great American revivalists such as Charles Finney, Billy Sunday, and Dwight L. Moody all preached the return of Christ to earth. So has the greatest revivalist of our own era, Billy Graham. He recently responded to a question about this very issue, saying:

> When Christ comes again—as He repeatedly promised to do—He will come through the heavens with glory and power, accompanied by a host of angels. All the earth will see His coming, and even His enemies will realize they have been opposing the Son of God.[8]

Throughout the twenty centuries since Jesus soared heavenward and that pair of white-clad messengers announced that He was traveling on a round-trip ticket, His followers of every persuasion have taken those angels at their word. Yes, on this one broad point there is remarkable unity among those who take the Bible seriously: Jesus Christ will return as He promised!

That, regrettably, is where the unity, harmony, and agreement abruptly end.

THE PROPHETIC PUZZLE

Practically from the very beginning of the church age disagreements surrounding the details and timing of the Savior's return began to divide believers and theologians into competing camps. Perhaps the most fundamental of these divisions sprang from how to interpret the biblical book that constitutes the centerpiece of eschatology—the Book of the Revelation of Jesus Christ. Throughout history theologians have tended to take one of three different views of John's apocalyptic visions.

One group, the preterists, assume most of the cataclysmic events described in John's narrative symbolically depict the events surrounding the siege and destruction of Jerusalem by the Romans in AD 70. Another, the historicist camp, views the visions as prophetic, symbolic references to the ongoing, unfolding story of the church and her battle with Satan through the centuries. The third group holds the futurist view. As the name suggests, this school of interpretation puts most of the events in John's visions into the future. And unlike the other two camps, futurists take John's visions literally wherever possible.

In recent years a fourth approach to the Book of Revelation has emerged. The idealist view of John's Apocalypse sees the book as an allegory depicting the ages-long conflict between good and evil in this fallen world. They view the book's role in the canon of Scripture as an encouragement to believers facing hardship or persecution in every era of history to stand firm and be confident in God's ultimate victory.

These wildly divergent views about the Book of Revelation have parallels in the ways Bible scholars view the millennium— that is, the thousand-year reign of the saints of God with Christ on the earth described in Revelation 20:4–6. (We will explore this topic in much greater depth later in this book.) You may have heard the terms *premillennial, amillennial,* and *postmillennial* used to describe these varying views.

Even among premillennialists—who stand in complete agreement about their approach to biblical prophecy and the nature of the millennium—we find three different views of *when* the rapture of the church will take place in relation to the seven-year tribulation period. Passionate debates about whether the catching away of the church occurs before, after, or in the middle of the prophesied seven-year season of global convulsion and woe have raged for decades. Internet forums frequented by evangelicals churn with lively, occasionally heated discussions of whether the Scriptures suggest that end-time believers will go through *all* of the tribulation period, *half* of it, or *none* of it at all.

For the most part all the advocates for these various positions love God, have our Lord Jesus in their hearts, and regard God's Word as their ultimate reference point for truth and light. Indeed, the participants in these debates all wave their Bibles in the air, saying, "Can't you read? It's so clear!" When I was a preteen, our living room was filled every Tuesday night, as my parents would invite pastors of differing interpretations to "share" them openly.

In the face of all this divergence of opinion is it any wonder so many among the rank-and-file believers in the pews on Sunday morning simply throw their hands up in despair of ever making sense of it? A theological mind no less formidable than that of the reformer John Calvin seemed to do the same.[9] He once said of the Book of Revelation, "Only God knows what this means."[10]

Perhaps God's plans for the culmination of history are not quite as open-and-shut as some would like to think. Maybe we should hold our preferred interpretations with open hands and hearts of humility. Perhaps a spirit of charity and grace should characterize our encounters with sincere believers who read it differently than we do. May I humbly submit that the body of Christ would be better served if every student and would-be teacher of Bible prophecy were to dial back the dogmatism a click or two where these things are concerned? The Internet has more than enough heresy hunters and self-appointed theology police.

Of course, I too have reached some conclusions about these questions, and I offer them on the pages that follow. A lifetime of study and prayer have led me to some firmly held views about how the Word of God should be interpreted where "last things" are concerned. *Interpreted* is the operative word in the previous sentence. Hear me clearly when I say Scripture is inerrant and infallible. Unfortunately we, and our capacities to interpret it, are flawed and not nearly so reliable. This is never truer than when we approach the Bible's prophetic, apocalyptic passages.

Early in my ministry I had the privilege of sitting at the feet of one of the twentieth century's great preachers and teachers, Dr. Lester Sumrall. My friend and mentor entered heaven in 1996 after more than six decades of astonishing impact, fruitfulness, and influence. He began his ministry as a fresh-faced seventeen-year-old in 1930. I recall him telling me about some of his early mentors and influences—silver-haired men of God who by the mid-1940s had already seen more than their share of convulsive world history. I vividly remember him laughing about how one of these veteran preachers said he and all his preacher friends were going to have to stop preaching about the end times because their surefire, rock-solid candidates for the Antichrist had all died on them. Every time they were sure they had identified the guy who fit the profile—Woodrow Wilson, Mussolini, Hitler, Pope Pius XI, Franklin Delano Roosevelt, and a number of others—the candidate was ushered off the stage of history by death.

I have filed Dr. Sumrall's story in a prominent spot in my memory as a cautionary tale about going too far in speculation about these things. What's more, the "Name the Antichrist" game is far from the only tempting trap into which teachers of Bible prophecy frequently fall. Christian history is littered with date setters whose confident predictions about the timing of the rapture—many based on meticulous calculations and painstaking research—proved to be fundamentally and embarrassingly flawed.

I hope you won't be disappointed to learn that I have no desire to add my name to that long list of red-faced prognosticators. I will not be outing the Antichrist and have no intention of predicting a date for anything. The mockers and scoffers of our age—the militant skeptics and postmodern cynics—have enough fuel for the fires of their derision without God's preachers handing them fresh kindling.

With those caveats in mind, I can tell you my studies have led me to a place of comfort and confidence concerning the basic timeline of the last days and what our response as believers should be to the events we see unfolding in Israel and around the world. You hold in your hands more than a guide to understanding a complex but important subject. This book is more than a hair-raising peek into what those who miss the catching away of the church will experience as our tired old spinning planet is turned inside out.

This is a road map for living victoriously and fruitfully in the volatile days leading up to our glorious departure. It is a guide for experiencing peace in the midst of our raging cultural storms. For the blood-bought, set-apart church of Jesus Christ, this can and should be our finest hour, and I intend to explain why.

I believe these insights are so very important in this moment of human history. In fact, the exhortations I am about to share are the same ones I deliver regularly to the wonderful people it is my privilege and sobering responsibility to shepherd.

I often bring these vital truths to the remembrance of my family and loved ones. I keep them constantly before my own heart and mind, and now I am bringing them to you. We must all—men and women, young and old—be as those fabled "sons of Issachar" among David's mighty men of valor: "having understanding of the times and what Israel should do."

I proclaim these truths boldly and passionately because I am troubled by the diminished place they hold in many pulpits across our nation today. A whole generation of believers has grown up in church without ever hearing, much less truly understanding, the promises, warnings, and exhortations embedded in the doctrine of the second coming.

I grew up in church during the sixties and seventies and

remember the Sunday night movie projector showings of *A Thief in the Night*. I vividly recall our youth groups singing the sobering song "I Wish We'd All Been Ready." In that day churches across the land sang songs such as "Jesus Is Coming Soon," "The King Is Coming," "The Eastern Gate," "Sweet Beulah Land," "He's Coming Again," "What a Meeting in the Air," and "Looking for a City." A bedrock staple of evangelical preaching was the message: "Look up! Jesus is coming again!"

I was taught to both look for and love the Lord's returning. So I have poured out onto these pages not only the detailed results of my years of study and prayer around this subject but also my deep and abiding passion for it.

This book also marks the completion of a trilogy examining the most significant events in the history of our world—the harrowing crucifixion, followed by the triumphant resurrection of our Lord and Savior, Jesus Christ. The first in this series emerged in 2013 with the publication of my deep exploration of Jesus's sacrificial death.

In *The Cross: One Man... One Tree... One Friday...* I revealed how Jesus's work on Calvary's cruel hill represents the axis of human history, the culmination of God's long grand strategy, thousands of years in the unfolding, to wrest back control of earth and man from the evil one. In *The Cross* I pulled back the curtain of the spirit world to reveal what was taking place at Calvary in the realm of angels and demons. Together readers and I stood in awe at the depth, breadth, and towering height of the Lamb of God's redemptive act—from the excruciating pain and suffering He willingly endured on that angry, mean, biting beam to His unwavering and immeasurable love for you and me and all of mankind.

Of course, Jesus's death was not the end of that Passover weekend's saving labors. One can't depict the horror and sorrow of that Friday and neglect the glory of Sunday. So the year 2016 brought the publication of *Gone: One Man... One Tomb... One*

Sunday.... That book revealed the resurrection as "the jubilee of the universe" and the zenith of God's brilliant redemptive strategy to legally restore what had been legally forfeited by Adam. I took readers on a profound journey to understand the great gulf between the first Good Friday and Easter. I invited them to discover how Jesus's victory over death marked the consummation of God's plan of the ages and revealed a glorious mystery hidden since the foundation of the world.

Yet this story is still incomplete, isn't it? The mighty footstool of God's grand redemptive plan of the ages rests on three golden legs, not two. The epic story of the Son of Man's quest to make a broken planet whole again demands three chapters in the telling.

Yes, God became man and laid down His guiltless life as a substitutionary sacrifice for a rebellious, orphaned race. Yes, He then conquered death and hell to swing wide the door to eternal life for every human heart willing to humbly step across that threshold and receive it. But what of that angelic promise to the eleven on that stony hillside some twenty centuries ago?

The third act of the greatest three-act drama ever conceived has yet to debut. As you're about to see, I believe the curtain is about to rise. What is certain, however, is that the script was written long ago. We will explore the details of the plot in the chapters that follow. It is a story of almost unimaginable scope and power. As with the previous two acts, this coming drama is built upon a promise.

There was God's Isaiah 51 promise to send the suffering Servant who would bear our sins, who would carry our sorrows, and by whose stripes we would be healed. He kept that promise.

Then there was His promise not to let His anointed One suffer corruption but rather would raise Him up on the third day. That promise too was kept in full.

We worship a faithful, promise-keeping God. And so we

await the fulfillment of a third, pending promise: "This same Jesus, who was taken up from you to heaven, will come in like manner as you saw Him go into heaven."[12]

Let us explore together the script for this third act.

CHAPTER 2

Untangling the Timeline

How vain therefore must be the presumption of those, who, in the light of their own understanding, would pretend to interpret this book.... There is no greater presumption than that of trying to understand this part of the word of God by any other light than that of the Holy Spirit.[1]

—BRITISH SEMINARY TEXTBOOK ON REVELATION (1841)

IT IS 9:39 a.m. on a Tuesday morning, and every newsroom of every major media outlet in America is a scene of utter pandemonium. News directors, writers, editors, reporters, and technical engineers are all shouting at one another or into phones while swarms of paper-carrying assistants and interns try to avoid colliding as they move back and forth across rooms at a dead run.

This was supposed to be a slow news day. The closest thing to a hot item on this morning's schedule of events was the president of the United States visiting an elementary school in Sarasota, Florida, and reading to some second graders. The date is September 11, 2001.

I am compelled to recall these events, first, because we never forget. I also describe them because my position as the founder of both Harvest Preparatory School and Valor Christian College offers me the privilege and duty to speak to a generation that, if born on that day of terror and infamy, would today be fifteen years old. None of them have a real-life memory of those horror-filled hours.

Similar scenes of chaos are playing out in other venues at precisely the same moment. These include FBI headquarters in Quantico, Virginia; inside New York Air Route Traffic Control Center on Long Island; on Air Force One, flying in a swarm of F-16 fighter escorts at forty thousand feet over America's heartland; and in the Emergency Operations Center in a bunker deep beneath the White House.

In each diverse locale the objective is essentially the same: to make sense out of chaos; to sort through a bewildering cascade of unanticipated and unimaginable events, figure out what is actually happening, and try to determine what might happen next and what to do about it.

For most the information avalanche began at 8:46 a.m. eastern standard time with reports of an explosion at one of the twin towers of the World Trade Center. This was followed immediately by unconfirmed reports that an aircraft had hit the North Tower. At this point several air traffic control centers have been hearing chatter about one or more possible commercial hijackings for more than twenty minutes. American Airlines headquarters got a call from a terrified flight attendant reporting the same.

Then, at 9:03 a.m., as dozens of live news cameras and hundreds of handheld video devices capture images of black smoke billowing from a gaping gash in the side of the North Tower, a commercial airliner screams into view and slams into the South Tower, producing a massive fireball. Over the next ninety minutes somewhere between one hundred and two hundred fifty trapped individuals will hurl themselves from the upper floors of the two towers. Witnesses on the ground look on in horrified disbelief, and cameras record for posterity.

As the minutes tick away, a relentless, dizzying stream of information continues to rush in[2]:

- "F-15 fighters from Otis Air National Guard Base near Long Island have been scrambled and are heading for Manhattan."

- Two minutes later: "More reports of hijacked airplanes."

- Four minutes later: "The FAA has just closed all New York City area airports."

- Three minutes later: "All the bridges and tunnels into and out of Manhattan have been closed."

- Five minutes later: "The FAA has just ordered a 'ground stop' of all civilian air traffic in the continental United States. All takeoffs have been canceled, regardless of destination."

- One minute later: "All military bases in the United States have just been ordered to elevate threat conditions to Force Protection Condition (FPCON) Delta, the highest state of alert."

- Eleven minutes later: "Eyewitnesses in Washington, DC, report hearing an explosion and seeing smoke rising from the general area of the Pentagon."

This is crazy. What is happening here?
Is America under attack? What is next?

Now the stream of new information from varying places, sources, and situations becomes a flood—each new bit more unexpected and appalling than the last. The twin towers collapse in turn, each sending multitudes on the ground running for their lives from an onrushing tsunami of gray ash, concrete dust, toxic chemicals, and atomized human remains that seems to be monstrously alive. A fourth hijacked airliner is down in a Pennsylvania field but is suspected to have been heading for the White House or the US Capitol. A shadowy group called the Democratic Front for the Liberation of Palestine calls a Middle East television network claiming credit. Intelligence community veterans suspect Osama bin Laden's organization instead.

For those various clusters of people struggling to get a handle on this day, the river of puzzle pieces—images, sounds, and information bits rushing in from scores of tributaries—gradually begins to form a blurry picture.

Of course, more than a decade and a half after the events of that day we all know the sequence well. Fever-browed conspiracy theorists aside, we all know not only *what* happened but *when*. We know not only the order of the events of 9/11 but also how those events connect and relate to one another. In other words, we understand the timeline. Of course, that is the power of hindsight.

Yet none of that was clear on that Tuesday morning as a horror story unfolded in real time.

Unlike the events of 9/11, and despite what you may have heard, the Book of Revelation is not a horror story—at least not for God's people. It is a victory story. It is a past-present-future account of overwhelming victory and glorious hope. Above all else, it is the story of the revealing of Jesus Christ.

Even so, the narrative it presents—its symbols, numbers, imagery, and events—can overwhelm and disorient any reader. This is obviously the case given the existence of all of the divergent interpretations I described in the previous chapter. Add to this the fact that most studies of the Book of Revelation, by necessity, expand to encompass the related prophetic writings of Daniel, Ezekiel, Zechariah, and others, not to mention the letters of Paul that touch on last things and the words of the Lord Jesus Himself concerning "the end of the age."[3]

For example, Revelation has its Beast. Elsewhere, John writes of an "antichrist."[4] Paul warns about the coming of "the man of sin," "the son of destruction,"[5] and "the lawless one."[6] Daniel prophesies of a boastful "little horn"[7] and later, "the prince who shall come."[8] Are these different but uniformly evil tyrants who appear on the world stage in different eras, or are all these references to the same individual? John mentions unusual creatures and signs in the heavens, along with seals, books, bowls and trumpets, angels, saints, martyrs, and elders. All of these and much more march and merge across the pages of the final Book of our Bibles.

Daniel chapter 9 speaks of "seventy weeks" (of years) and "one week" (of years), and chapter 12 speaks of "time, times, and half a time," whereas the Book of Revelation references a tragic period of 1,260 days in chapters 11 and 12, and then in chapter 13 a period of woe lasting forty-two months. Do these various methods of counting three and one-half years all refer to the same period? And is this the same season the prophet Jeremiah called "the time of Jacob's trouble"?[9]

Like those frantic reporters in their newsrooms on 9/11, many believers struggle to organize and make sense out of seeming confusion and disorder, sorting through a bewildering cascade of unimaginable events in an effort to figure out what is actually happening, and to thereby discern what might happen next.

We need a timeline. A timeline brings order to pandemonium. It serves as the picture on the lid of the puzzle box, letting you know what the chaotic jumble of pieces looks like when correctly assembled. Over the next few chapters I will offer just such a timeline.

Again, this is not a horror story leading us all to a frightful, grim, and appalling conclusion. Yet some who revel in the task of interpreting it treat it as such.

In our perverse culture people flock to horror and disaster movies. Carnage sells. The higher the body count, the bigger the box office haul, it seems. Some people appear drawn to the Book of Revelation's narrative for similar reasons. Global cataclysm accompanied by death counts in the hundreds of millions are anticipated with a sort of giddy delight. I'm reminded of a line from one of the Batman movies describing the motivations of the super villain: "Some men just want to watch the world burn."[10]

Others squander untold hours in intensive speculation about the identity of the Antichrist, employing elaborate mathematical systems equating certain names with the number 666. In a similar vein every new technology discovered is invariably declared to be the one that ushers in "the mark of the beast" mentioned in Revelation chapter 13. In my lifetime Social Security numbers, binary computer code, product bar codes, RFID chips, QR codes, and smartphones have all been candidates or precursors to this "mark." Some sort of advanced technology will almost certainly be involved, but I'm convinced such speculation is poor stewardship of precious time and energy.

All of this misses the point at two levels. First, as the timeline I am about to present indicates (spoiler alert!), none of these individuals or systems will be obvious while the church of Jesus Christ remains on the earth. They only reveal themselves after God's people have been caught away. Far too many believers are fretting, dreading, and feverishly preparing themselves for a tribulation they will never see. Frankly I'm weary of seeing God's precious and powerful saints living in terror, trembling, and trepidation concerning the state of the world and their future in it. This is completely unnecessary and inappropriate for sons and daughters of the coming King, the one and only Creator of heaven and earth, and Lord and Ruler of all.

Secondly, I believe passionately that we can and should approach our study of the Revelation of Jesus Christ with positive expectancy and reverential joy. In fact, it is the only book that promises a reward for those who read it: "Blessed is he who reads and those who hear the words of this prophecy…"[11]

Perhaps more than any other New Testament book it is helpful to understand the context and setting of the Book of Revelation's writing. Let's begin our journey toward a clarifying timeline by examining the background and birth of the Bible's most mysterious and misunderstood book.

Ruling like a queen over the blue-green Aegean Sea sits the ancient, cosmopolitan port city of Ephesus. She is a brilliant jewel embedded on the eastern arc of the Roman Empire's circular Mediterranean crown. The shining centerpiece of this proud city is the white-columned Temple of Artemis. It—along with other architectural wonders such as the Great Pyramid of Giza, the Hanging Gardens of Babylon, and the Colossus of Rhodes—will one day be considered one of the "Seven Wonders of the Ancient World." Artemis, the Greek goddess of the hunt, along with her Roman equivalent, Diana, is revered and worshipped in magnificent temples all over the Roman world. But none rival the splendor and intimidating presence of her shrine in Ephesus. Pilgrims from across Rome's dominion travel here to sacrifice and implore her favor. It has stood here for more than four centuries and will stand three centuries more.

Yet the shrine of Artemis is far from the only magnificent pagan temple here in the heart of Ephesus. This wealthy center of international trade and commerce boasts dozens of opulent pagan temples from a variety of pantheons. For example, centuries of trade with Egypt has endowed Ephesus with a large Egyptian population. Thus we find in the middle of the governmental district a pink granite temple dedicated to the Egyptian goddess Isis.

A theme is emerging here—namely, goddess worship. Clearly the demonic spirits of goddess-centered idolatry are deeply entrenched in this place. In fact, ancient Greek legends reaching back into misty antiquity suggest the city was originally founded by the Amazons, a mythical tribe of fierce female warriors.

Even so, not all the temples in Ephesus honor female deities or even ancient gods. Some of the most recent additions to the cityscape are temples and monuments dedicated to the worship of mortal men—specifically Roman emperors.

The first of these was erected for Julius Caesar, who had transformed the ancient Roman Republic into a dictatorship. Following his death in 44 BC, he was declared to be *divus*—that is, divine, a god—and a temple in Ephesus was erected to facilitate his worship. Julius's son Octavian succeeded him and didn't wait until death to make himself an object of worship like his father. He changed his name to *Augustus*, a title connoting majesty and near-divinity, and allowed the title "Son of God" to be attributed to him by his supporters and sycophants. Augustus also positioned himself as a semi-divine mediator between the Roman people and Rome's gods—offering sacrifices on their behalf as a type of high priest. Coins were struck declaring him to be "savior of the world" and other messianic phrases.

The successors of Caesar Augustus followed suit. Each new emperor claimed more god-like power and demanded more devoted worship than did his predecessor. For example, debauched and demented Nero, whose blood-soaked rule of the Roman Empire ran from AD 54 to AD 68 and contained the first widespread persecution of Christians, ultimately began encouraging comparisons between himself and the sun god, Apollo.[12] Both Peter and Paul are believed to have been martyred under this tyrant. This growing and increasingly mandatory governmental cult went far beyond declaring, "Caesar is king." It demanded a profession that "Caesar is Lord."

By the AD 90s cities such as Ephesus were filled with temples, markers, and monuments urging worship of the Roman rulers. Even so, Rome's citizens and subjects still enjoyed a narrow form of freedom of religion. That is, one could worship whatever god or gods one chose, providing one *first* acknowledged the lordship of Caesar. It was on this point that a new, rapidly growing movement of the followers of Christ constantly ran afoul of the Roman government. These Christians' stubborn refusal to acknowledge any Lord but Jesus Christ continually put them in the crosshairs of an all-powerful messianic state.

Many Bible scholars regard the birth date of the bride of Christ as the day of Pentecost and her place of birth, Jerusalem. This was fifty days after the Passover sacrifice of the Lord Jesus, in which He once and for all time fulfilled the role of the old covenant's Passover lamb, and ten days after His ascension into heaven. From Jerusalem this new, radical faith began to spread—first throughout Judea, then Samaria, and soon to the uttermost corners of the Roman world. Even so, for the first several decades of the movement's existence, Jerusalem served as its wellspring, anchor, and center of gravity.

That all changed in AD 70 when the armies of the Roman general Titus laid siege to Jerusalem to crush a Jewish revolt. Much of the church at Jerusalem fled into the Syrian Desert. Meanwhile the city was utterly destroyed. Herod's magnificent re-creation of Solomon's Temple was burned, and not one stone was left upon another—just as Jesus had prophesied to His disciples.[13]

By that time the apostle John had already been based in Ephesus for some time—having brought Mary, the mother of Jesus, to live with him there.[14] Paul had ministered there extensively as well. As a result of their efforts most of the major cities of Asia Minor harbored thriving Jesus communities. These included seven significant cities connected by a semicircular

Roman road running from Ephesus into the interior of the province. From Ephesus an itinerating apostle could travel north on that road and pass through Smyrna and Pergamum. From there the circuit-riding preacher could head southeast on that road through four other cities—Thyatira, Sardis, Philadelphia, and Laodicea. These cities were regional centers of influence in themselves.

For all these reasons Asia Minor became the center of gravity for Christianity in the Roman Empire after the devastation of Jerusalem. Ephesus suddenly found itself the hub of the fledgling faith's ever-expanding wheel. Only the church in Rome rivaled it for influence.

A vibrant, growing establishment of Christianity in a place so saturated in idolatry did not take place without incident, however. The entire nineteenth chapter of Acts chronicles Paul's introduction of the Jesus movement (as well as an introduction to the baptism of the Holy Spirit) to the people of Ephesus.

Acts 19:21–41 records an extraordinary incident connected with the Temple of Artemis in Ephesus. Apparently the Christian faith was growing so rapidly in Asia under Paul's preaching there that the local craftsmen, whose livelihoods centered upon the selling of likenesses of the goddess, began to feel a threat to their wallets. One leader among them, a silversmith named Demetrius, got the entire guild worked up into a violent frenzy, which then snowballed into a massive angry mob in the center of the city. At that point many of the participants weren't all that sure what they were rioting about. They did know they were supposed to be outraged and that it had something to do with that odd sect of Jews, their infamous refusal to honor "proper" gods, and the teaching of this group's primary spokesman and advocate, Paul of Tarsus.

Doctor Luke's account reveals that at one point the seething throng drowned out all attempts to reason with them by chanting, "Great is Artemis of the Ephesians!" at the top of their lungs continuously for two hours. Eventually cooler heads prevailed and the mob dispersed without further incident.

Luke's narrative serves as a revealing glimpse of the tense and volatile context into which the church of Jesus Christ had been planted in this Roman province. Several decades after that incident the most recent in the dynastic line of Roman emperor gods decided he would stamp out the Jesus movement once and for all.

Domitian's rule begins in AD 81, although an assassin's dagger will bring it to an abrupt end in AD 96. Rome has been in decline and disarray, so the emperor has initiated an empire-wide campaign to restore it to its former glory. A key element of this program involves bringing into line this mysterious movement that has spread through the empire for the last sixty years like some sort of viral infection. Domitian is determined that these "Christians" will either demonstrate their patriotism by acknowledging the primacy of the emperor cult or be purged. This demonstration often involves submitting an incense offering and swearing an oath at one of the many designated Caesar-worship temples.

Across the empire those rumored to be believers in Jesus are dragged before tribunals and ordered to profess their worshipful adoration for the emperor. Those who refuse, or who openly profess to be Jesus's followers, are either quickly executed in some horrifying fashion or sentenced to be worked to death as slave laborers at one of the empire's numerous mines or quarries that dot the islands of the Mediterranean Sea. The Romans have a name for the latter option. It is *damnati in metallum*, Latin for "condemned to the mines."

Thousands of courageous saints are sent to Sardinia, off the western coast of Italy, to die in that island's numerous silver and lead mines. Others die quarrying and moving marble from the multitude of islands dotting the Aegean Sea. Among these is an island called Patmos. It lies roughly twenty miles southwest off the coast of Ephesus. Laboring among the *damnati in metallum* there on this craggy, barren hellhole is a gaunt, silver-haired man well past his ninetieth year. His name is John. He is earth's last living member of Jesus of Nazareth's original inner circle.

Strange rumors about the old man swirl and circulate among the Roman guards. Some say he can't be killed. It's certainly true he has, inexplicably, already outlived younger, stronger prisoners who arrived at the same time. One persistent story says the Roman governor of Asia had him dropped into boiling oil a few years ago and that this leader of the Christians simply walked away from it as if it had been a warm bath! Although unsure about the accuracy of those reports, the guards tend to give the ancient apostle a wide berth, just to be safe. This includes allowing him some time alone on his strange religion's special day of worship—the one the prisoner calls "the Lord's Day."

Jesus Revealed

The theme of this Book is found in its opening sentence, "The Revelation of Jesus Christ." This should be borne in mind from first to last, and our object should be to see Him as He is here revealed.[1]

—G. Campbell Morgan (1863–1945)

I was in the Spirit on the Lord's Day...[2]

So explains John in the opening chapter of his book we call Revelation. I frequently hear the name of the final book in our Bibles treated as a plural, "Revelations." The unspoken implication here is that the book is a collection of strange visions, or *revelations*, recorded by John. This misses the vital point of the book. The inspired writer himself gives us the full, proper title in the opening words of his letter:

The Revelation of Jesus Christ...[3]

This book reveals Jesus. It is not a revelation of the devil. It is not a revelation of fear, dread, or despair. No. It offers you and me, the readers, a perspective of our Lord and Savior we have previously not enjoyed. This is an extraordinary privilege not unlike the one granted Peter, James, and John when they were invited to accompany the Master up to the "mount of transfiguration." There a curtain is pulled back to reveal a dimension of their friend and leader they had not dreamed existed. Matthew writes, "[Jesus] was transfigured before them. His face shone as the sun, and His garments became white as the light. Suddenly Moses and Elijah appeared to them, talking with Him." [4]

As I have already stated, we should approach this book with excitement and expectancy. To read it is to be granted an insight not afforded to those who neglect it. Zacchaeus, short of stature, climbed a sycamore tree for only a fleeting glimpse of the Savior as He passed by. The Book of Revelation, on the other hand, offers us exceedingly more than a mere glimpse. In its pages we connect with a vivid, panoramic, multidimensional presentation of the King of Kings in His unmatched splendor. Is it any wonder, then, that the opening lines of John's book promise a blessing to those who read and heed it? [5] Christian, our encounter with John's final word should be met with joy rather than trepidation. We're about to receive a blessing!

The opening chapter of Revelation is essentially a cover letter explaining why John is sending it to the seven churches of Asia Minor. After some introductory remarks, in which John points out that he is writing to "the seven churches which are in Asia," he explains how he came to receive the content he is about to share in the rest of his letter:

> I, John, both your brother and companion in the tribulation and kingdom and patience of Jesus Christ, was on the isle that is called Patmos on account of the word of God and the testimony of Jesus Christ. I was in the Spirit on the Lord's Day, and I heard behind me a great voice like a trumpet, saying, "I am the Alpha and the Omega, the First and the Last," and "What you see, write in a book, and send it to the seven churches which are in Asia: to Ephesus, Smyrna, Pergamum, Thyatira, Sardis, Philadelphia, and Laodicea." [6]

You surely have noted that these seven churches correspond to the previously mentioned seven cities that lie along a main Roman road into the interior of the province. It would not be difficult for a letter to make its way from Patmos to Ephesus.

Supply ships constantly made their way back and forth on the twenty-mile sea journey. From there a single courier could easily be dispatched from Ephesus with copies of John's letter and have them in the hands of the elders of those churches within a few days. From these strategically located cities additional copies could then be made and distributed through the province and on to the wider world.

After hearing the "voice like a trumpet," John wheels around and is stunned to see nothing less than the dazzling presence of the King of Kings Himself. But this is not the meek, approachable carpenter from Nazareth now standing before John in the midst of seven golden candlesticks. This is not the familiar friend upon whose breast John once reclined at dinner. No. The Son of Man John knew now stands before him as the Lord of Glory:

> The hair on His head was white like wool, as white as snow. His eyes were like a flame of fire. His feet were like fine brass, as if refined in a furnace, and His voice as the sound of many waters. He had in His right hand seven stars, and out of His mouth went a sharp two-edged sword. His appearance was like the sun shining brightly.
> —REVELATION 1:14–16

Not surprisingly this sight wrecks the beloved disciple. He collapses in a heap of fear, reverence, and awe. But even now the Great Shepherd's first impulse is to calm and comfort His troubled sheep. He puts a gentle hand on the quivering man's shoulder and says, "Do not be afraid. I am the First and the Last. I am He who lives, though I was dead. Look! I am alive forevermore. Amen. And I have the keys of Hades and of Death."[7]

These words of reassurance are immediately followed by

instructions. In them our Canaan King gives us a major down payment to that timeline we need. He says:

> Write the things which you have seen, and the things which are, and the things which will take place after this.
> —REVELATION 1:19

This directive provides the overarching framework for everything that will follow. It reveals that this book is arranged into three sections:

- Things that John has seen (the past)
- Things that are (the present)
- Things that will take place later (the future)

As we move forward in the book, it will become clear that Revelation chapter 1 represents the things John has seen. Chapters 2 and 3, containing the letters to the seven churches, constitute the "things which are." The balance of the book—chapters 4 through 22—reveals the "things which will take place after this." This third section is obviously the largest portion of John's message, and it is in this long leg of the journey through Revelation that many readers get lost, confused, or simply overwhelmed. We'll spend most of our time there, but before we do, we would do John a disservice if we didn't at least briefly explore the two preceding chapters.

Again chapters 2 and 3 represent the "things which are." As we have already noted, the seven cities cited are real, existing communities at the time of John's writing. A real local congregation overseen by a real pastor existed in each of these cities in Asia Minor. John had almost certainly been providing apostolic oversight to these congregations during his years of living in Ephesus. Thus, it is no surprise at all to find him receiving messages from the Bridegroom to pass along to these seven components of His bride.

Jesus makes this clear in the final verse of chapter 1:

> The mystery of the seven stars which you saw in My right
> hand, and the seven golden candlesticks: The seven stars
> are the angels of the seven churches, and the seven can-
> dlesticks which you saw are the seven churches.
> —REVELATION 1:20

Many Bible scholars believe the "angels" referred to by the
Savior very well may be a reference to the pastors of those
congregations. The Greek word translated *angel* in the New
Testament simply means messenger. In any event the seven distinct and specific exhortations John is commissioned to deliver
here are, first and foremost, real instructions custom tailored
for real local churches facing real, distinctive circumstances.

This does not mean, however, that there isn't a wider meaning
and a broader application in these seven messages. In a similar
way many of the Old Testament prophecies had an immediate
or contemporary application while simultaneously finding fulfillment in the distant future. There is abundant, vital truth for
us in each of these mini-epistles—truth that will set us free.
Furthermore some interpreters of Revelation have seen conspic-
uous parallels between the characteristics and circumstances of
these seven churches and seven distinct phases of church history. In other words, they see the congregation at Ephesus as
representing the early church. A few centuries later the church
as a whole entered a phase of resembling the church at Smyrna.
Following this logic the church at the end of the age would have
the characteristics of the "lukewarm" congregation at Laodicea.

Whether this is accurate or not, it is clear that all these
messages are part of Holy Scripture, and as such they are as
relevant and as powerful as a two-edged sword for you and
me today. This section of your Bible is "inspired by God and
is profitable for teaching, for reproof, for correction, and for

instruction in righteousness, that the man of God may be complete, thoroughly equipped for every good work."[8]

All seven messages follow a pattern, a template of sorts. Each begins by identifying the congregation being addressed.

To the church in Thyatira, write...

To the church at Philadelphia, write...

Each also contains a different title or symbolic description of the Lord Jesus that hearkens back to John's initial description. To Ephesus He is "He who holds the seven stars in His right hand, who walks in the midst of the seven golden candlesticks" (Rev. 2:1). To Smyrna He is "The First and the Last, who was dead and came to life" (v. 8). To Pergamum He is "He who has the sharp two-edged sword" (v. 12). To Sardis He is "He who has the seven spirits of God and the seven stars" (Rev. 3:1).

Allow me to pause for a moment to invite you to rejoice with me that Jesus Christ is still "He...who walks in the midst of the seven golden candlesticks." Those candlesticks represent the churches or individual congregations that make up the global, universal church of Jesus Christ. You see, our churches are designed to be broadcasters of light in a dark and darkening world. Each church is a candlestick or lamp. And this title reveals Jesus's moving among them. Christian, He is present; He is in our midst! He walks among us still, urging us to shine and dispel as much darkness as possible!

Each church letter also contains a specific message with three parts: (1) a commendation, (2) a condemnation or correction, and (3) an exhortation.

It is both noteworthy and sobering that in six of these seven churches Satan had made inroads in some form or another. One church he was able to destroy completely. And only one of the seven remained untainted by his defiling, corrupting presence. I am sometimes haunted by this harsh mathematical reality as I drive the streets of America's cities and see a church on virtually every street corner. Does that six-to-one ratio still hold for churches today? I pray not, but I am concerned that it may.

From Revelation chapter 4 forward we are in the third segment of John's remarkable letter. We are about to see the "things which will take place after this." In other words, through the telescope of prophecy we will gaze into the future.

A source of unnecessary confusion for some readers of these remaining chapters is the fact that as we look through John's eyes at a series of astonishing sights, our perspective changes several times. Some scenes take place on earth, while others take place in heaven. Occasionally the narrative jumps from one place to the other with little or no warning. It is a bit like my preaching style, so buckle up; it's going to be quite a ride.

Chapter 3 closes with a somber encouragement directed not only to those seven churches of Asia Minor but also to you, to me, and to all believers everywhere and in every time. Jesus declares, "He who has an ear, let him hear what the Spirit says to the churches."[9]

> *Father in heaven, grant us ears to hear what Your Spirit is speaking to us in this pivotal hour of human history!*

Chapter 4 clearly signals a major shift in the narrative. John gives the cue, "After this I looked. And there was an open door in heaven." Then he hears that penetrating and unmistakable trumpet-like voice again:

> Come up here, and I will show you things which must take place after this.
>
> —Revelation 4:1

Please note the command, "Come up here." It is an unam-
biguous indicator that our perspective is about to be redirected
from earth to heaven, but it is more than that. It is a type of,
a symbolic foreshadowing of the catching away of the church,
more commonly referred to as the rapture. Let's *selah* that for a
moment—that is, let's ponder it. John is on earth when instantly
and unexpectedly the glorified Son of God appears. His voice
bellows, "Come up here," and immediately John finds himself
standing in heaven with an unanticipated and overwhelming
view of the flawless throne room of Jehovah God Almighty.

Here John stands proxy for all the redeemed of planet earth,
living and dead, who will one happy day, perhaps one day very
soon, hear that trumpet-like shout and be immediately caught
up to heaven.

> For the Lord Himself will descend from heaven with
> a shout, with the voice of the archangel, and with the
> trumpet call of God. And the dead in Christ will rise
> first. Then we who are alive and remain shall be caught
> up together with them in the clouds to meet the Lord in
> the air. And so we shall be forever with the Lord.
> —1 THESSALONIANS 4:16–17

We will explore this extraordinary event in much greater
detail in the chapters ahead. For now may I simply exhort you,
dear reader, to look up! When you look down, you only see
where you are, not where you are going. Determine now to
refocus your gaze. Choose to look above and beyond your current circumstances and the calamitous absurdities of this fallen,
broken, hurting world. Lift your eyes toward the eastern sky!
Set your affection on things above, not on things below.[10] Are
you watching? Are you waiting? Are you anticipating?

Yes, in the opening verses of chapter 4 our Redeemer releases
a shout, and John is caught away into the presence of God:

> Immediately I was in the Spirit. And there was a throne
> set in heaven with One sitting on the throne!
> —REVELATION 4:2

Immediately! In a moment! In a twinkling of an eye! Such was the suddenness of John's transport from earth to heaven, and such will be our experience on that grand day.

It is important to note the placement of this "rapture." It takes place just as John is about to be shown a series of cataclysmic events that clearly fall within a seven-year period of sorrow and judgment upon the earth. As we will see, that seven-year span neatly divides into halves. Three and a half years of "tribulation" are followed by another three and a half years of even more intense activity known as "the great tribulation."

First we see John's symbolic, representative "rapture." Only then do we see tribulation upon the earth. This settles it for me. That great company, the people of God, His church, will be caught up to heaven and will remain there in the presence of the Lord as horrible judgments are poured out and as the four horsemen of the apocalypse gallop across the landscape.

This is the reason I find it impossible to join those well-meaning believers who work themselves into a panicky lather about whatever the one-world utopians and new age social engineers are plotting this week. I simply cannot bring myself to fret, wring my hands, cower, hunker down, "prep," dig in, or in any way forfeit my blood-bought peace and joy. The price He paid was simply too high for that. John is caught up into heaven before those seals of calamity are broken, before those bowls of judgment start tipping and spilling, and before those four apocalyptic horsemen saddle up. I'm satisfied that well before the vile Antichrist makes his diabolical entrance upon the world stage, I, along with all those redeemed by faith in the living Christ, will hear the Captain of the hosts of heaven, the God of the angel armies, shout, "Come up here!" Less than a second later we will be enjoying the same unspeakably awesome sight that greeted John that day.

What did he see?

> And there was a throne set in heaven with One sitting on the throne! And He who sat there appeared like a jasper and a sardius stone. There was a rainbow around the throne, appearing like an emerald. Twenty-four thrones were around the throne. And I saw twenty-four elders sitting on the thrones, clothed in white garments. They had crowns of gold on their heads. Lightnings and thunderings and voices proceeded from the throne. Seven lamps of fire were burning before the throne, which are the seven Spirits of God. Before the throne was a sea of glass like crystal.
>
> —REVELATION 4:2–6

John is permitted to survey the very throne room of the Most High, Creator of heaven and earth. Never before had a human been privileged to behold such a scene. Several things John notes at this point are significant and full of revelation.

A rainbow surrounds the throne. This quickly reminds us of the post-flood promise made to Noah, recorded in Genesis 9:13, which directs us both to God's covenantal faithfulness as well as to the reality that sin demands judgment. In His righteousness and holiness the Creator built our universe upon the bedrock of a judicial framework. Sin, if not accounted for by an atoning sacrifice, *must* result in judgment. As I explained in great depth in my book *The Cross: One Man... One Tree... One Friday...*, this is precisely why the Lord Jesus had to come, live a sinless life, and die upon Calvary's cruel hill. This is also why John is about to witness judgment poured out upon a Christ-rejecting world while he, representing all redeemed humanity, observes safely from heaven's portals.

John recorded seeing twenty-four elders assembled at the throne. This detail is rich with symbolism. Here we have the number twelve and multiples of twelve appear at least 163 times in Scripture (NASB). It is a figure that throughout Scripture speaks of the perfection of God. We are instantly reminded of the heads of the twelve tribes of Israel and the twelve apostles of the Lamb. Here we have the old covenant saints with the new covenant saints. They are all arrayed in all-white robes, indicating they have been washed in the blood of Jesus Christ. Their crowns are of gold, and they are seated with the Ancient of Days. They represent all of redeemed mankind and are privileged to occupy the best seats in the house for both observing and participating in the most extraordinary worship service ever held.

Next John speaks of seven "lamps of fire," which he reveals to be "the seven Spirits of God." This I believe to be a reference to the Holy Spirit in seven unique manifestations. How is this possible? How can the singular Holy Spirit of God be said to have "seven Spirits"? The prophet Isaiah may have offered us some insight into this paradox:

> The Spirit of the LORD shall rest upon him, the Spirit of wisdom and understanding, the Spirit of counsel and might, the Spirit of knowledge and of the fear of the LORD.
>
> —ISAIAH 11:2

Here Isaiah reveals several distinct manifestations of the singular "Spirit of the Lord":

1. Wisdom
2. Understanding
3. Counsel
4. Might
5. Knowledge
6. Fear of the Lord

Finally John relates that "before the throne was a sea of glass like crystal." In prophetic language *seas* and *clouds* are often used to describe innumerable throngs of people. (See Isaiah 17:12; Jeremiah 51:42.) Often such prophetic "seas" are depicted as being turbulent and chaotic. Yet the vast sea of humanity before the throne of God is revealed as being like glass. Speaking of the perfect peace resting upon those who make up this glorious sea, they abide in magnificent calm and are at rest.

Notice the term *crystal* is also in John's description of the numberless throng of the redeemed assembled before God's mighty throne. Crystal is known for its clarity. No impurities or defects can go undetected in crystal. Please remember how Paul admonished the Ephesians that Jesus Christ was ever and always cleansing His bride with His Word, "that He might present to Himself a glorious church, not having spot, or wrinkle, or any such thing, but that it should be holy and without blemish."[11] This crystal sea is a holy convocation. We know they're holy and pure because crystal reveals all blemishes. This numberless multitude has been washed, and that washing has made them spotless!

Midway through the fourth chapter John the revelator redirects his attention, and ours, to four extraordinary "living creatures" located near and around the throne. Each is fantastically different, yet all four have commonality, having six wings and being "covered with eyes all around." These great guardians of the throne also lead worship in heaven. In a type of call-and-response, which was common in many churches a generation ago, the four creatures cry out, and the twenty-four elders answer:

> All day and night, without ceasing, they were saying:
> "'Holy, holy, holy, Lord God Almighty,' who was, and is, and is to come."
>
> When the living creatures give glory and honor and

thanks to Him who sits on the throne, who lives forever and ever, the twenty-four elders fall down before Him who sits on the throne, and worship Him, who lives forever and ever. Then they cast their crowns before the throne, saying,

"You are worthy, O Lord, to receive glory and honor and power; for You have created all things, and by Your will they exist and were created."

—REVELATION 4:8–11

Believe me, it is not quiet in heaven, and I can't wait to add my voice, my clap, and my shout to the celebration of worship! Can you imagine it? I will be there, and so will you if you have accepted Jesus Christ as your Savior. What a thought! What a privilege to stand with that blood-bought multitude. I don't have to be near the throne. Just allow me to be a part of that crystal sea! Grant me the unspeakable privilege of standing among the redeemed of the Lord when the twenty-four elders begin to cry, "Holy, holy, holy!"

Until that day we can still sing:

> Holy, holy, holy! All the saints adore thee,
> Casting down their golden crowns around the glassy sea;
> Cherubim and seraphim falling down before thee,
> Which wert, and art, and evermore shalt be.[12]

This exalting and exhilarating worship service for the ages brings chapter 4 to a close, and chapter 5 opens with the next event in John's throne room vision. This and the next fifteen chapters depict the events of the tribulation and the great tribulation. The earth trembles, and her remaining inhabitants experience seven long years of cataclysmic judgment outpoured as the restraining influence of believers is withdrawn from the world of men.

In the subsequent chapters the physical, visible return of

Jesus Christ to this planet as well as the establishment of His thousand-year earthly reign are published. Next the final judgments appear, along with the ultimate disposition of Satan and all of his fallen angels. Then we step into eternity.

Thus we have a simple, easy-to-grasp timeline for the events vividly described in the Book of Revelation:

- The present church age
- The rapture
- Seven years of tribulation (comprising two three-and-a-half-year segments)
- The return of the King of Kings to earth—that is, the second coming
- The thousand-year reign of Christ on earth (the millennium)
- The final judgment
- Eternity

Now with the *timeline* simplified, we turn our attention to the *timing*. The next great event on God's prophetic calendar is the catching away of the church. Let's explore the key signs that direct us to, if not the day and hour, at a minimum the season of this glorious milestone.

Dry Bones Live Again

*Israel has now become alienated from her own land. Her sons,
though they can never forget the sacred dust of Palestine, yet die at
a hopeless distance from her consecrated shores. But it shall not be
so forever. . . . If there be anything clear and plain, the literal sense
and meaning of [Ezekiel 37:1–10]—a meaning not to be spirited
or spiritualized away—must be evident that both the two and
the ten tribes of Israel are to be restored to their own land.*[1]

—CHARLES H. SPURGEON (1834–1892)

The bones are the whole house of Israel.—Ez. 37:11-12

ISLAMIC CLERICS ASSURE the faithful that there has never
been a Jewish temple on the Jerusalem hill commonly known
as the Temple Mount. The imams claim Solomon's Temple and
Herod's Temple are simply myths and fabrications. Only Muslims, the Quranic theologians assert with a straight face, have
ever worshipped on the hill in Jerusalem on which today sits
the Al-Aqsa Mosque and the shrine known as the Dome of
the Rock.

It's an absurd claim, but it is not hard to understand why
Islamic leaders make it. In the political, and occasionally military, tug-of-war over the most ancient section of that venerable
city the plain details of history don't exactly help their case.

Even so, in April 2016, with very little fanfare or notice in
the media, a powerful arm of the United Nations essentially
sided with imams—repudiating a fundamental tenet of both
Judaism and Christianity and rewriting an entire chapter of
ancient Roman history in the process. A gaggle of international

bureaucrats "erased" more than a thousand years of accepted history that included any Jewish/Israelite connection to the Temple Mount.

The perpetrator of this deceptive and audacious feat was the United Nations Educational, Scientific, and Cultural Organization (UNESCO), which deals with cultural heritage sites. On April 11, 2016, UNESCO's fifty-eight-member executive board met in Paris and overwhelmingly passed a resolution that effectively denied the validity of two major world religions by recognizing only Islam's connections to that holy, history-rich site.

The resolution, titled "Item 19—Occupied Palestine," condemns Israel for "abuses that violate the sanctity and integrity" of a Muslim holy place. The text of the resolution repeatedly referred to the site only as "Al-Aqsa Mosque/Al-Haram Al Sharif." In fact, the only reference to any Jewish connection to the ancient complex in the five-page document is a single mention of the "Western Wall Plaza" (with the scare quotes in the original document) and comes only after identifying the famous remnant of the second temple as Al-Buraq Plaza, an Arabic designation honoring Mohammed's horse![2]

That's right—a United Nations agency voted to revise history. Apparently David never conquered a Jebusite stronghold on that hill in the tenth century BC or made it the new capital of the unified Israelite tribes. Nor did his son Solomon ever build a magnificent temple there to house the ark of the covenant.

Because it never existed, that temple didn't remain the center of Jehovah worship for the next four hundred years until being overrun and dismantled by Babylonian armies. Despite what you may have heard, an exile named Ezra did not return seventy years later with a commission from the Persian king Cyrus the Great to begin reconstruction of that temple. And despite mountains of written and archaeological evidence, King Herod the Great, one of the most ambitious builders of the first century BC, never undertook an opulent renovation and expansion of what is universally known as the second temple. Sure, in his memoirs the Roman general Titus distinctly remembers laying siege to Jerusalem and ordering his men to level that temple, but he was clearly confused.

How exhilarating it must be to be vested with the power to sweep aside centuries of accumulated academic, archaeological, and anthropological data with a show of hands and the stroke of a pen. Such is the amazing power of a United Nations agency.

In response to the UNESCO vote Israeli Prime Minister Benjamin Netanyahu issued a passionate statement that included this fiery denunciation:

> UNESCO ignores the unique historic connection of Judaism to the Temple Mount, where the two temples stood for a thousand years and to which every Jew in the world has prayed for thousands of years. The UN is rewriting a basic part of human history and has again proven that there is no low to which it will not stoop.[3]

For the record, only six countries—Estonia, Germany, Lithuania, the Netherlands, the United Kingdom, and, thankfully, the United States—opposed this nefarious resolution, while thirty-three supported it, and all others abstained. Such is the world in which we now live. This is a world not only in which there are many who wish Israel did not exist but also in which some are attempting to pretend it never did.

In the final days of His ministry leading up to His sacrificial death, the Lord Jesus pulled His disciples aside to speak to them about His coming kingdom. In the course of that conversation, recorded in Luke 17:20–37, the disciples asked several key questions about His return. The most obvious of these questions, human nature being what it is, was, "When will these things come to pass?"

Jesus responded by laying out a number of warnings and indicators. But in the final verse of that discourse, verse 37, the disciples voiced another question. They asked not when but *where*:

> They asked, "Where, Lord?"
> He replied, "Where the body is, there the eagles[4] will be gathered together."

Yes, it's one thing to ask Jesus what signs to look for that indicate His return is near in *time*. It's another thing altogether to ask Him what exact location! This constitutes quite a question, considering the earth encompasses one hundred ninety-seven million square miles. Talk about a needle in a haystack! Our Savior's answer may seem a bit cryptic at first glance. "Where the [dead] body is, there the eagles [or vultures] will be gathered together." What does that mean?

Jesus is saying there will come a time when the attention of every nation will be drawn to a specific geographic location on the map. That point, my friend, is a nation no larger than the state of New Jersey, tenaciously clinging to the edge of the Mediterranean's eastern coast, kissed daily by its azure waves. Yes, Jesus said "where" is the key to the "when." So we must draw our attention to that shimmering diamond on the velvet couch of history. We must fasten our attention on the spot that for millennia has served as the crossroads of three continents and the collision point of world empires in conflict.

Of course, I'm talking about Israel, and, more specifically, its ancient capital, Jerusalem. Jesus admonished them, and us, to watch the nation of Israel. Yet this is quite the paradox because for most of the last nineteen centuries there was no Israel to watch! Believers throughout that era seeking to heed the Lord's instructive words assumed He must have been speaking metaphorically or of some invisible, *spiritual* Israel. An exiled people scattered to the four winds for centuries couldn't possibly suddenly reassemble and become a nation once again, could they?

Even so, in the 1800s the Spirit of God began to whisper to those with hearing hearts and a knowledge of His Word about a future restoration of Israel. The mighty preacher Charles Spurgeon was one of these discerning souls.

As early as 1855 he exhorted his congregations with insights such as these:

> The hour is approaching, when the tribes shall go up to their own country; when Judea, so long a howling wilderness, shall once more blossom like the rose; when, if the temple itself be not restored, yet on Zion's hill shall be raised some Christian building, where the chants of solemn praise shall be heard as erst of old the Psalms of David were sung in the tabernacle....*I think we do not attach sufficient importance to the restoration of the Jews.* We do not think enough about it. But certainly, if there is anything promised in the Bible it is this. I imagine that *you cannot read the Bible without seeing clearly that there is to be an actual restoration of the children of Israel....*For when the Jews are restored, then the fullness of the Gentiles shall be gathered in; and as soon as they return, then Jesus will come upon Mount Zion with His ancients gloriously, and the halcyon days of the Millennium shall then dawn; we shall then know every man to be a brother and a friend; Christ shall rule, with universal sway.[5]

Spurgeon saw in the Bible what increasing numbers of others would begin to see in the decades that followed. A restoration of Israel was coming, and when it came, it would be a sign of some very important things to follow.

Two massive tsunamis of Roman military might crashed down upon Israel—the first in AD 70, a second and final blow in

AD 130—washing the surviving Jewish population out of their ancestral, God-granted homeland and into the remote corners of the world.

The Lord Jesus, wrapping Himself in the mantle of the final old covenant prophet to Israel, had repeatedly warned His Israelite hearers that this was coming. Notice the riveting words of Jesus in Matthew's Gospel, chapter 23:

> O Jerusalem, Jerusalem, you who kill the prophets and stone those who are sent to you, how often I would have gathered your children together as a hen gathers her chicks under her wings, but you would not! Look, *your house is left to you desolate.*
> —MATTHEW 23:37–38, EMPHASIS ADDED

This sobering prediction of gathering destruction comes at the end of a long, thundering, prophetic discourse in which Jesus pronounces seven "woes" upon the scribes and the Pharisees. The desolation our King predicted for Jerusalem's house came almost forty years to the day later. In other words, the very same generation that heard the Messiah's grim prophetic warning witnessed its awful fulfillment.

A few days before Passover in AD 70 the armies of general and future Roman emperor Titus surrounded the city, severing it from the outside world. Three Roman legions amassed on the western side of the walled and fortressed city. A fourth dug in for a long siege across the Kidron Valley on the Mount of Olives to the east. The city was filled to overflowing with Jewish pilgrims, there to observe the first of the three Jewish pilgrimage feasts.

During the months-long offensive campaign those who attempted to escape the city were captured and crucified. The Jewish historian Josephus reveals in his book *The Jewish Wars* that the Romans slaughtered so many in this way that they eventually ran out of wood for crosses. He goes on to estimate that as the walls of Jerusalem were breached and the battle-hardened centurions poured in upon that half-starved population, roughly 1.1 million died by the sword. Nearly one hundred thousand were enslaved and transported to points throughout the empire.

The devastation of Judea, her capital, and the shimmering gold and white temple at its heart was unfathomable. Not one stone was left upon another, just as the Lord Jesus had prophesied.[6] Yet in the decades that followed, successive Roman emperors began rebuilding parts of the city, and Jewish people began to straggle back and inhabit it. Then in AD 130 another uprising against Roman rule brought the wrath of the empire down upon the city once again. Another siege and slaughter ensued. This one concluded with the mass suicide of nine hundred sixty Jewish holdouts in a mountaintop fortress called Masada. Any surviving Jews of Judea were exiled and forbidden to ever even enter the city of Jerusalem on pain of death. This Roman ban on any Jewish presence in the Holy City, David's Citadel, would remain intact for the next three hundred years.

Even following the collapse of the Roman Empire the land of Israel would remain under the control of a succession of gentile powers—pagan, Christian, and Muslim. Byzantines, Saracens, Roman Catholic Crusaders, Ottoman Turks, and other cultures each trod Jerusalem underfoot for their season. Meanwhile, century after century, the exile of the Jewish people continued. They remained scattered among the nations of the world like wandering, drifting, disconnected stars on the backdrop of an ebony sky.

No temple. No city. No country. No true *home*. Yet even though they were hated, feared, and persecuted wherever they were cast amid the vast global *diaspora*, the Hebrews persisted as a distinct people. They were seemingly engineered by God Himself to resist assimilation into their surrounding cultures, and that stubborn refusal to assimilate only fueled the suspicions and resentments of the darker minds around them. Only the providential hand of God kept the world's Jews from being destroyed through prejudice and oppression. This remained the state of world affairs year after year and century after century. Then the turbulent twentieth century arrived, and something implausible, unthinkable, and impossible occurred. This miracle had been previewed by an exiled Judean prophet around the year 600 BC!

In the thirty-seventh chapter of Ezekiel the prophet records an extraordinary vision. The Spirit of the Lord transports him to a desolate valley, the floor of which is carpeted with piles of human bones. These are not the bodies of the recently deceased. They were bleached white by the sun and have been here a very long time. The prophet observes that the bones are "very dry."[7] Then, as the astonished prophet is still processing the shocking scene before him, the Ancient of Days asks him a question.

"Son of man, can these bones live?" Ezekiel is no fool. His cautious, tactful reply is, "O Lord GOD, You know."[8]

God then commands Ezekiel to prophesy to this tangled sea of skeletal remains. The Lord reveals His desire to put flesh back on these old bones. So Ezekiel complies, and as he does, the valley suddenly echoes with the sound of rattling as scattered bones reassemble themselves and then begin to take on muscle, cartilage, and flesh. Then an instructive command is given: prophesy to "the four winds."

> Then He said to me, "Prophesy to the wind; prophesy, son of man, and say to the wind: Thus says the Lord GOD: Come from the four winds, O breath, and breathe upon these slain so that they live." So I prophesied as He commanded me, and the breath came into them, and they lived and stood up upon their feet, an exceeding great army.
>
> —EZEKIEL 37:9–10

What an astonishing vision. But what was the meaning? If Ezekiel hadn't already guessed, his answer was quickly forthcoming:

> Then He said to me, "Son of man, *these bones are the whole house of Israel.* They say, 'Our bones are dried up, and our hope is lost. We are cut off completely.' Therefore prophesy and say to them, Thus says the Lord God: Pay attention, O My people, I will open your graves and cause you to come up out of your graves *and bring you into the land of Israel.*"
>
> —Ezekiel 37:11–12, emphasis added

Here our magnificent artist Jehovah God paints a vivid, unforgettable picture of miraculous restoration before Ezekiel's watching eyes. Actually *resurrection* is a better term. A prophetic word is spoken, and suddenly a dead, dry, scattered, disassembled thing is reassembled and brought back to life. It begins with God's asking, "Can these bones live?" It ends with God's declaring, "These bones are the whole house of Israel."

For nearly nineteen centuries the nation of Israel was effectively dead. The homeland was a desolate, barren husk of its once vibrant self—a habitation for little more than wild animals and wandering bedouin. It was as Spurgeon called it in his day: "a howling wilderness." Her once proud people were scattered to the terminus of every compass point. Then in the fullness of time the Lord God gathered His royal robes and stood to speak. All of heaven hushed to hear what the Ancient of Days would declare and decree. On another occasion this same Jehovah had stood over a vast, dark, cosmic void and said, "Light, *be*," and suddenly light *was*. Now every angelic ear strains in anticipation of what might proceed from the lips of the Most High on this hallowed occasion. Then the divine word comes:

"Dry bones, *live!*"

No sooner had these words left the mouth of the Creator than a rattling sound was discerned across planet earth. Jews from every nation, on every inhabited continent, were suddenly filled with an indescribable, irresistible longing for a place they had never even seen, much less visited. Men and women whose families had lived in the same spot for hundreds of years suddenly uprooted themselves and moved to a remote, desolate backwater region that nobody wanted or cared about until Jews decided they wanted to live there.

God prophesied once more, and the breath of His mouth caused a wind to blow across that land. Suddenly, in the twinkling of an eye, a new country was born, taking its rightful place among the ranks of the world's sovereign nations.

Do you have a dry bones valley in your life today? God wants to speak to those dead and disconnected places and bring divine restoration.

You can rely upon the promises of a faithful God today. Don't ever, ever doubt them. What prevailing hope lives in the hearts of those who are convinced that not one line of His Word will ever fall to the earth void of power! He holds all things together even now by the power of His Word! Hear Him speak: "Heaven and earth will pass away, but My words will never pass away."[9]

Trust it, my friend. Learn it. Lean upon it. Love it every moment! Live it every day! Each promise is an oak of God planted in the forest of eternity, entwining its roots around the Rock of Ages.

The very existence of Israel is a sign to you and me today. But it is more than a sign. It is a forerunner. What happened physically and materially in Israel first, will happen spiritually in the church of Jesus Christ. Do you see it? He's going to breathe His mighty breath upon the dry, lifeless bones of dry and dying churches again. A great revival is coming to the church. I know this because He said He was returning for a spotless bride. I know it because He is the God who transforms a valley inhabited by only dry bones into a living, breathing, conquering army.

We have already examined Jesus's fiery prophetic sermon recorded in Luke chapter 17, warning of impending judgment of the scribes and Pharisees. We find its parallel passage in Matthew chapter 23.

The Savior delivered this message in the courtyard of the temple itself. Matthew 24 picks up with Jesus and the disciples departing the temple complex on their way to His favorite place of refuge far from the noise and dust of the city: the Mount of Olives. On the way there one of the disciples speaks admiringly of the stunning temple architecture. Jesus replies by saying, in essence, "Take a good, long look, men. A day is coming when not one of those stones will be left upon another. They will all be pulled down."

When they arrived at the Mount of Olives, the disciples were bursting with questions for their leader concerning His shocking proclamation. Matthew consolidates them into a single, three-part query:

> Tell us, when will these things be, and what will be the sign of Your coming and of the end of the age?
> —Matthew 24:3

Notice they inquire of Him what will be the *sign*, singular, not *signs*, plural, of His coming and the end of the age. They are asking, what is that one, singular sign that alerts the vigilant that the return of our Canaan-conquering, crucified, resurrected King of Glory is imminent? What is the *sign* of His coming?

In response Jesus first gave them several developments to look for as precursors and forerunners of that primary sign. It's a chilling list that includes wars, famines, epidemics, and earthquakes. Yet He immediately adds, "For all these things must happen, but the end is not yet.... All these are the beginning of sorrows."[10]

The beginning of sorrows. Now there is a sobering phrase for you. Of course, skeptics are quick to point out that every generation throughout history has seen more than its share of wars, famines, pestilence, and natural disasters. This is true and precisely why near the end of His discourse Jesus gives the master sign—the one indicator that makes all the others relevant:

> ⌐Nation of Israel
> Now learn this lesson from the fig tree: When its branch becomes tender and grows leaves, you know that summer is near. So also, when you shall see all these things, you know that it is near, even at the doors. Truly I say to you, this generation will not pass away until all these things take place.
>
> —MATTHEW 24:32–34

The fig tree frequently serves as a prophetic symbol for the nation of Israel throughout Scripture. You will recall that Jesus cursed a fruitless fig tree, and it withered from the ground up (Matt. 21). This was a chilling and symbolic indictment of the hypocrisy of Israel's leaders and a stern warning of the coming desolation.

Now our Savior suggests that when you see the fig tree come back to life following a long winter of barrenness, you can "know that it is near, even at the doors." His point is that a time of desolation is coming to Israel, but when Israel comes back to life, you will know that the time is at hand.

The historical record testifies that a trickle of Jews began making their way back to their ancient homeland in the late 1800s. Then what became known as the Zionist Movement was officially born in 1897. Suddenly Jewish people all over the world were discussing the need for an official homeland, preferably in the land God had originally granted to their fore-father, Abraham.

One of the most significant outcomes of World War I, which raged from 1914 to 1918, was the transfer of control of much of the Middle East from the Islamic Ottoman Empire to Christian Great Britain. This rapidly increased the flow of Jews returning to the land of promise from a trickle to a stream.

A second world war paved the way for the miraculous restoration of Israel as a nation. When the appalling depth and breadth of Hitler's Holocaust became known at the end of World War II, the entire world recoiled in horror. The Zionist Movement's long campaign among the governments of the world for permission to establish a tiny but permanent homeland in historic Judea and Samaria gained instant traction as opposition withered.

The British left Palestine on May 14, 1948, and modern Israel declared itself a sovereign nation that same day. That familiar blue and white flag emblazoned with the ancient Star of David was raised over a reborn Israel. It was unthinkable, utterly implausible, mathematically incalculable—and yet it happened.

What is that there on the shores of the Mediterranean? Could it be? No. Impossible! That ancient, lifeless fig tree, barren for nineteen centuries—why, it's budding! It's putting forth leaves!

The sign that makes all the other signs relevant suddenly appeared for the entire world to witness. It signals one thing: a great transition is about to begin.

CHAPTER 5

Labor Pangs and the Great Transition

*I hope that the day is near at hand when the advent of
the great God will appear, for all things everywhere are
boiling, burning, moving, falling, sinking, groaning.*[1]

—MARTIN LUTHER (1483–1546)

"The beginning of sorrows."

THAT IS HOW the Lord Jesus described it in Matthew 24:8,
referring to the signs in the earth that the Bridegroom's
appearing to catch away His bride was imminent. Among these
were wars, famines, epidemics, and natural disasters. As we saw
in the previous chapter, these signs were only relevant if they
appeared after, or in concert with, the master sign—the rejuve-
nation of the fig tree, Israel.

That sign appeared for the entire world to see in 1948. The
improbable, the implausible, the unthinkable happened. After
nineteen centuries of exile, dispersion, persecution, ostracism,
and wandering, the Jewish people not only maintained their
racial and religious identity, but they also found their way home.

The Roman emperors who sought the utter destruction of
both Israel and the Jewish sect known as the Christians are
mere footnotes in dusty, unopened history books. Today we
name our dogs Nero and our sons Paul. Meanwhile the standard emblazoned with the blue Star of David snaps and pops
in the breeze that billows across the sacred soil God granted
Abraham three millennia ago.

Where are those once mighty empires that dominated the land God expressly granted to Abraham and his descendants? They were brought to nothing. All are scattered and bleaching in the sun across the refuse heap of human history.

The prophet Daniel foresaw the rise and fall of world powers that would dominate Israel. He had a remarkable dream, recorded in Daniel chapter 7, that told of great events in world history—and most of them have already come to pass exactly as God showed him they would. For instance, the empires of Babylon, Persia, Greece, and Rome have all passed into antiquity. (See Daniel 7:1–7.)

The reason I said *most* of the things Daniel saw have happened is because the time of fulfillment for some of the things he saw prophetically has not come yet, but I believe it is near at hand. And I am convinced the things that have not occurred as yet will come to pass just as certainly as the things that have.

The last portion of chapter 7 is an explanation by an angelic interpreter of the meaning of Daniel's dream—especially regarding the appearance and behavior of a ruler who was distinct from the others and who was "warring with the saints and prevailing against them" (v. 21). This is none other than the Antichrist, as he is identified in Revelation. But the good news is that even so long ago judgment was determined upon this world ruler who would presume to oppose God and oppress His people:

> But the court shall sit for judgment, and they shall take away his dominion, to consume and to destroy it forever. Then the kingdom and dominion, and the greatness of all the kingdoms under the whole heaven, shall be given to the people of the saints of the Most High, whose kingdom is an everlasting kingdom, and all dominions shall serve and obey Him.
>
> —DANIEL 7:26–27

Adolf Hitler sought the destruction of the Jewish people as he boasted of a Third Reich that would last for a thousand years. A few fleeting years later he died raving, drooling, and whimpering in a desolate Berlin bunker, abandoned by all but his mistress. You cannot take a world map and point out to me the present location of the Third Reich. But you can look on that same map and show me where the apple of His eye has been miraculously regathered!

Israel *is*. Israel stands. Israel prevails! As I write these words, descendants of Jacob walk the ancient stone pavements of Jerusalem, just as the Bible promised they would! Prayers in Hebrew rise up from synagogues all over the land of Jesus's birth. The anointed psalms of the shepherd boy David grace the lips of schoolchildren.

Yes, the fig tree has blossomed. King Jesus prophesied that Israel would be left desolate but would be a nation once again at the time of His return. And it has! Yet there are even greater promises shouting to us from God's immutable Word. It indicates that the Jewish people will be worshipping God in their temple on Temple Mount. When He appears, the temple will be rebuilt, and the sacrifices commanded of God through Moses will be offered once again. Clearly that piece of the prophetic picture has not yet fallen into place.

As I pointed out in the previous chapter, the rocky plateau once crowned with Solomon's Temple, and centuries later Herod's magnificent re-creation of it, is currently occupied by the Al-Aqsa Mosque and the Dome of the Rock. Jews are scarcely allowed to walk on Mount Zion and are forbidden to pray on that holy hill.

Even so, across Israel plans and preparations are quietly under way to restore the worship of Jehovah there. Architectural drawings for the third temple have already been finalized. Garments for the priests, meticulously crafted in accordance with the exacting specifications of the Levitical instructions, are already hanging in the closet. The utensils of worship pre-scribed by God Himself in the time of Moses and Aaron have been painstakingly reconstructed.

Of course, a full and complete restoration of temple ministry will require priests to carry out the daily sacrifices—but not just any Jew from any tribe can serve as a priest in God's holy order. God Himself specified the tribe of Levi as the one from which the priesthood would come. Nor can just any Levite carry out the intricate duties of temple sacrifice. Leviticus chapters 8 through 10 stipulate that this honor falls to a specific branch of the Levite tribe—the descendants of the "sons of Aaron."

How can this possibly happen? It has long been assumed that all traces of Jewish tribal identity had been lost amid the Holocaust and the countless dispersions, persecutions, genocide, and forced relocations the exiled Israelites suffered through the centuries. No Jewish person could say with confidence from what tribe he or she hailed. This appeared to be an insur-mountable obstacle for the restoration of authentic temple wor-ship. Then came the increasingly sophisticated science of DNA testing. How unsearchable is God's wisdom and how mar-velous are His ways!

In the late 1990s researchers conducted genetic analyses on Jewish men from various locations around the world. The testing revealed that Jewish men carrying the surname Cohen—a common family name in Jewish communities worldwide—tended to carry an unusual genetic marker in common. Ancient Jewish tradition associates the name Cohen with the *Kohanim*, the descendants of Aaron.

That's right; numerous genetic studies of modern-day *Kohanim* have provided scientific evidence supporting the oral tradition of an ancient priestly lineage that survives to this day. Certain Jewish men carry a characteristic on their Y chromosome—the genetic information passed from father to son. In the technical terms of the science of genetics this marker is called the Cohen Modal Haplotype.[2]

All you and I need to know is that the descendants of the ancient priesthood of Aaron can now be genetically identified, and as a result a mountainous barrier to the recovery of temple worship has been uprooted and cast into the sea. Yet this is not the only obstruction to those making preparations for temple restoration on Mount Moriah.

Once potential members of a priesthood have been identified, assembled, and trained, they must be ritually purified prior to carrying out a single duty in any new temple. The instructions God delivered to Moses require such purification to be accomplished in part with the ashes of a very specific type of cow, a "red heifer."[3]

For several decades now Israeli rabbis, livestock husbandry experts, and geneticists have been quietly working together to breed an unblemished red heifer that would satisfy the biblical requirements, which are exceedingly stringent. For example, any red heifer born with even two hairs of another color is disqualified! Scores of promising red heifer candidates have been put forth with breathless excitement in recent years, but each has eventually been rejected. Yet they are tantalizingly close. Not many days from now a perfect specimen will be born, and yet another giant leap toward the fulfillment of this ancient prophecy will have been taken.

This flurry of preparation for constructing a third temple on the very same hill Jesus walked upon when He graced Herod's Temple with His pristine presence presents an obvious question: What about the revered Muslim sites currently occupying the site where that temple must be built? I will address that thorny question in a later chapter.

For now let us bask in the exhilarating reality of where we currently stand in relation to God's prophetic timetable. As we have seen, two great end-time prophecies must be fulfilled before the physical return of Jesus to planet earth. The first is the restoration of Israel to the land of promise. The second is the reclamation of Jehovah worship at a rebuilt Jerusalem temple.

Clearly the former has already been fulfilled. As we've just seen, the latter is tantalizingly near.

The Greek word translated "sorrows" in our Lord Jesus's statement regarding the "beginning of sorrows" is *odin*. It is a word most commonly used by Greek speakers of Jesus's day to describe the pains of childbirth. Thus some Bible translations, such as the New American Standard Bible, render this verse, "the beginning of birth pangs."

As any mother can attest, the onset of labor is a clear signal that a shift is about to take place. It begins with little more than a simple feeling of uneasiness or a general sense of discomfort. The expectant woman simply can't seem to get comfortable. Then comes a nearly irresistible impulse to prepare. Some call this the nesting instinct. A transition of enormous significance is under way. My lovely wife, Joni, rearranged all the furniture in our home not once but twice at 2:00 a.m. during this phase in one of her pregnancies.

Then the first contractions start—short, mild, and well spaced. These progressively grow in duration, intensity, and frequency.

Something very similar is happening among God's people at this moment. Do you sense it? The uneasiness of living in this fallen, defiled place? The inability to get comfortable with the direction things are heading in our world? A growing longing for another, better place? An impulse to be busy about the King's business?

Do you understand that current conditions in the world around us simply cannot continue unabated without a significant shift? There must be a great transition. Even a casual observer with a modicum of understanding of biblical things can recognize that the signs of the end of the age are everywhere around us. The back page of your Bible reads like the front page of your city newspaper. The inescapable fact is that the great transition is already under way. In short every true believer is experiencing a divine drawing—a longing for home.

Home. I recently had the opportunity to go back home, but not to the place of my birth, nor of my current residence. I journeyed to my ancestral home—to Appalachia, the place of my people. The streams, hollows, and deep, dark hills of eastern Kentucky summon me in the deep recesses of my country-boy soul.

Whether it is the mountains ablaze with autumn's majesty or a rustic house clinging to a hillside, these are the sights of *home*. Whether it is the fragrance of a freshly mown field or fatback frying in a black iron skillet, these are the smells of *home*. Whether it is the hometown harmony of a gospel quartet or a coal truck in low gear laboring up the mountainside, these are the sounds of *home*.

These are the things indelibly imprinted on our souls that draw us back to our roots. These are the things that have helped make us who we are. We see it in our hearts, and we see this same drawing toward home reflected in a myriad of ways throughout the natural world.

Let the haunting, honking call draw your eye upward in spring and catch a glimpse of a V-shaped formation in the sky. The great Canada geese orient themselves by the earth's electromagnetic field, and with necks outthrust and wings outstretched, they sail northward to build their nests in the place of their nativity. There's no place like home.

For most of the year the silver salmon swims in the open sea. Yet at just the appointed time, guided through the pathless ocean by impulses they do not understand but simply obey, they head homeward to the stony brook of their birth. As I said, there's no place like home.

Even the horse, humbled by bridle and bit, can be broken of virtually every bad habit. Yet as any good horseman will tell you, if you give him his head and he catches a glimpse of the barn, he will soon be headed at full gallop to the comfort, safety, and familiarity of his stall because, you see, there really is no place like home.

Dorothy, with her little dog, Toto, made those words a permanent part of the Western cultural vernacular when she uttered them in the 1939 classic movie *The Wizard of Oz*. You know the story well. The two of them were transported by a tornado to a land beyond time where they witnessed wonders, passed through perils, and encountered companions who propelled them toward their primary purpose. They simply wanted to get back home.

When Dorothy awakened, her wish had come true. She opened her eyes surrounded by the people she loved and the familiar sights and smells of *home*. Then she uttered the words now indelibly etched on the consciousness of an entire generation: "There's no place like home."

It's true. Whether home is a plush penthouse, a tattered tent, a millionaire's mansion, or a country cabin, there truly is no place like home.

- Home—where your family welcomes you
- Home—where your friends remember you
- Home—where there is provision for every need
- Home—where there is protection from every attack
- Home—where there is healing for every hurt

- Home—where you can, as an old country
  preacher once said, "feel like you're somebody
  when you know you ain't nobody!"

And if you are a child of the living God, this world is not your home. Many songs have been written over the years about the longing for our true home in heaven. The apostle Paul clearly had this aching and longing in view when he wrote:

> We know that the whole creation groans and travails in pain together until now. Not only that, but we also, who have the first fruits of the Spirit, groan within ourselves while eagerly waiting for adoption, the redemption of our bodies.
>
> —ROMANS 8:22–23

Here is that Greek word *odin* again, this time rendered as "travails in pain." Here Paul employs language that describes the entire earth in the volatile throes of overwhelming change. When labor reaches its highest point of intensity, a transition is fully under way. It is as undeniable as it is unstoppable. My friend, we and this planet are headed for a great transformation.

Now your Bible is clear. This impending transition will be a time of trouble on earth never seen, witnessed, or experienced before. The four horsemen of the apocalypse—the Antichrist, War, Famine, and Death—gallop unrestrained upon the earth, no longer constrained by the preserving, moderating influence of the Spirit of God. Rivers turn to blood. Serpents, beasts, plagues, hail, fire and vapor of smoke, wormwood and blood moons strike terror into the hearts of countless millions. The seas, seething under the whiplash of fury, spill their dead into the lap of God. Man-made superhighways of steel-reinforced concrete flap like ribbons in a noonday breeze as the very earth itself shudders and convulses. The Antichrist and the False Prophet briefly step onto the stage, and the mark of the Beast—the number of his name, 666—makes its appalling appearance.

Yes, the full-blown onset of labor will include all these things. Yet, as I have already made clear, God's people will not remain on earth to suffer their tortuous torment, nor even to witness them. As Paul admonished his friends in Thessalonica, "God has not appointed us to wrath."[4]

All the signs indicate that we are about to be transported, in a moment, in a twinkling of an eye, into the paradise and presence of God. So shall we forever be with the Lord! We will be home. As your Bible exhorts, be comforted with these wonderful words.

There is no doubt the day is approaching when Jesus Christ will come to earth to rescue Israel from the hand of all those who seek her destruction. The first time, He came as the suffering Servant and was rejected by His people in accordance with the grand plan of God to extend salvation to the gentiles. When He comes the next time, He will be accepted and hailed by the Jewish people as their Messiah and conquering King.

Jesus had this in view when He said to all of Israel, "Look, your house is left to you desolate. For I tell you, you shall not see Me again until you say, 'Blessed is He who comes in the name of the Lord.'"[5] Paul saw it too and did his utmost to explain it to the gentile church in Rome:

> For I do not want you to be ignorant of this mystery, brothers, lest you be wise in your own estimation, for a partial hardening has come upon Israel until the fullness of the Gentiles has come in. And so all Israel will be saved, as it is written: "The Deliverer will come out of Zion, and He will remove ungodliness from Jacob"; "for

this is My covenant with them, when I shall take away their sins."

—ROMANS 11:25–27

God said Israel would be reborn. It is now a proud member of the nations of the world. God said the temple would be rebuilt in Jerusalem. Plans for its construction are nearly complete. And just as certainly God declared that our Lord Jesus Christ would split the eastern sky and physically and visibly return to this planet.

This is the "second coming." Yet many believers conflate this event with the sudden, stealthy catching away of the church—that is, the rapture—which occurs precisely seven years earlier. At His appearing in the heavens at the rapture, gravity will lose its hold upon us, and we will meet our Lord in the air, where He is suspended above the earth. At His second coming we're going to come riding back with Him as He literally steps back upon this fallen planet. Don't be concerned—this is all about to become much clearer.

CHAPTER 6

Rapture Ready

*I never lay my head on the pillow without thinking that perhaps before
the morning breaks, the final morning may have dawned. I never
begin my work without thinking that He may interrupt my work
and begin His own. This is now His word to all believing souls, "Till
I come." We are not looking for death, we are looking for Him.*[1]

—G. Campbell Morgan (1863–1945)

ACCOMPANY ME TO the eastern edge of Kentucky to a
lovely green hillside in Martin County. This hill stands
watch over a big horseshoe-shaped bend in the Tug Fork River
dividing Kentucky and West Virginia. Scattered there amid
the spring wildflowers, under the generous, cooling shade of
ancient oaks, we find several tidy rows of headstones. Note
those weathered granite slabs. They mark some precious territory for me.

May I tell you of an uncle of mine who, even as a youth, sang
and preached like a herald angel from another world? I believe
the ministry with which God has graced me would have been
his had he survived. But at the tender age of nineteen, with
one foot in manhood and one still in boyhood, Danny went
to serve his nation in the rice paddies of Vietnam. He found
his way home less than a year later in a flag-draped coffin. His
body rests here in the soil of this rocky hillside. Yes, this is hallowed ground.

Just over a bit farther is the marker for Grandmother Mimi,

the mightiest Christian it has ever been my privilege to know. Her spirit long ago moved on to her eternal reward, but the weathered shell that housed that lovely spirit for so many years is in repose here on this little hillside too.

I will also tell you of my sister, Debbie, who possessed the strongest faith I have encountered in all my years of Christian service. As a young mother-to-be, six months pregnant, my precious sister had a severe automobile accident that she and my unborn niece miraculously survived. Nevertheless it left Debbie struggling with debilitating health issues and excruciating pain for many years to follow. In 2007 she surrendered, and her spirit joined Mimi and Danny in that jubilant crystal-sea throng assembled before the jeweled throne of heaven. We brought her frail body back here, and here her earthly tabernacle awaits the reunion with her glorified spirit and soul.

In 2013 my father and best friend, James (or Clyde, as his family and friends lovingly called him), departed this earth for his heavenly home to join the rest of those who awaited him there. He too was laid to rest on that beautiful Kentucky hillside. To this day I can't express how much I miss him, and I am looking forward to the day when I can be reunited with him and all of my dear family and friends who have gone on before me.

No doubt you have your own place of hallowed ground. They are quiet places where the earthly bodies of believing loved ones have been laid to rest. Some of these, such as Grandmother Mimi and my father, may have lived long, full lives of service to the King. Others, such as Danny and Debbie, may have seen their journeys cut far too short.

I have good gospel news for you. As Mahalia Jackson used to sing, a "Great Gettin' Up Morning" is coming! Paul saw it:

> For this we say to you by the word of the Lord, that we who are alive and remain until the coming of the Lord will not precede those who are asleep. For the Lord

> Himself will descend from heaven with a shout, with the voice of the archangel, and with the trumpet call of God. And the dead in Christ will rise first. Then we who are alive and remain shall be caught up together with them in the clouds to meet the Lord in the air. And so we shall be forever with the Lord.
>
> —1 Thessalonians 4:15–17

The extraordinary event the great apostle describes is commonly referred to as the rapture. Skeptics are quick to point out that this word does not appear in Scripture. True enough, and yet they must agree that the concept appears throughout your Bible, the passage above being but one example. This is the catching away of all living saints to meet King Jesus in the air. Paul makes clear that this extraordinary event will be immediately preceded by the resurrection of the righteous dead. "And the dead in Christ shall rise *first*," he said.

If you and I were actually standing on that little Martin County, Kentucky, hillside right now, you might hear me shouting to those graves, "Get up, Debbie! Come on, Clyde! Hurry up, Mimi! Let's go, Danny! Because I can't be caught up until you're raised up!" Yes sir, yes ma'am, there is a "Great Gettin' Up Morning," when we will fare well.

There is not a single unfulfilled prophecy standing between us and this extraordinary event. Without a doubt resurrecting the bodies of His saints is the next item on God's prophetic agenda. But you and I will be right behind them. Paul was clear: "Then we who are alive and remain shall be caught up together with them in the clouds to meet the Lord in the air."[2]

Notice the location of this long-anticipated reunion. We meet our Savior "in the air." As I mentioned at the end of the previous chapter, more than a few people are confused on this point. Many mistake the rapture of the church for the second coming of Jesus Christ. It is a mistaken yet common assumption that these two terms describe the same event, when in reality they are two distinct events separated by a "week" of years.

At the biblical event we refer to as the rapture the Lord Jesus appears in the air and sky. At His second coming He proceeds through the air, clouds, and sky to actually place His feet once again on the earth. At the rapture only those who are born again are going to hear that trumpeting voice and see His appearance. At the second coming every eye will see Him. At the rapture Jesus comes *for* the saints. At the second coming He comes *with* the saints. At the rapture His appearing signals impending war and destruction on the earth. At the second coming His appearing signals the arrival of peace and restoration.

As I have made clear, I believe the preponderance of biblical evidence points to a rapture that takes place immediately *before* the seven-year tribulation period. The brief, momentous season of history that immediately follows our catching away has been reserved by God for conducting His final, redemptive dealings with the nation of Israel.

Among such evidence is the intriguing fact that the church is never mentioned in the Book of Revelation after chapter 3. As we have seen, chapters 2 and 3 are filled with direct messages from the Lord Jesus to the church. Then John is suddenly, without warning, "called up" to heaven, and the church is never addressed again. Why? Before John begins his startling description of the cataclysmic events of the seven-year period known as the tribulation, the church is already with the Lord in heaven.

Consider the words of Jesus in the light of what you learned in the prologue of this book concerning Jewish betrothal customs. Do you recall how the bridegroom would go away to build the dwelling place for the bride, often by adding rooms to the father's house? Surely the Lord had these customs in mind when He said:

> Let not your heart be troubled. You believe in God.
> Believe also in Me. In My Father's house are many
> dwelling places. If it were not so, I would have told you. I
> am going to prepare a place for you. And if I go and pre-
> pare a place for you, I will come again and receive you to
> Myself, that where I am, you may be also.
>
> —JOHN 14:1–3

Jesus declared that He was going away to prepare a place
for His bride, and He did. In the same breath He promised
that He would return. Will our Bridegroom be any less diligent about keeping that sacred, covenantal commitment to us,
His betrothed?

The role of the bride is to eagerly anticipate the Bridegroom's
return. Do we? Are we watching? She set herself apart, keeping
herself undefiled and her wedding garments spotless. Have we?
Are we merely *in* this fallen, sin-saturated world, or have we
gradually become *of* it? I must remind us of three rhetorical
questions Paul the apostle posed to the believers at Corinth.
"What fellowship has righteousness with lawlessness? And what
communion has light with darkness? And what accord has
Christ with Belial?"[3]

As members of the bride of Christ we eagerly watch, wait,
and anticipate. Meanwhile, back at the Father's house, the
Bridegroom is making His glorious preparations. When will
the lovesick Son be released to bring His beloved home? Only
when the Father gives the signal:

> Concerning that day and hour no one knows, not even
> the angels of heaven, but My Father only....Watch there-
> fore, for you do not know what hour your Lord will come.
>
> —MATTHEW 24:36, 42

If the Son Himself doesn't know the exact timing of His
return, then you and I certainly are not, nor need we be,
privy to that information. We, the bride, must do our due

diligence—keep our lamps filled with the oil of the Holy Spirit and be vigilant, for our Bridegroom may appear at any moment.

Frankly we all need a little more "at any moment" in our theology. An "at any moment" mind-set keeps one from treating one's spouse improperly or defrauding one's employer out of time and money.

We might worry less, pray more, sacrifice, serve, and share the love of God with our lost neighbor if we truly understood the imminence of His appointed appearing. I'm positive that we would spend more time looking up than with our countenance cast down.

The expectant bride keeps herself spotless. As Ephesians 5:27 describes it, His goal is "that He might present to Himself a glorious church, not having spot, or wrinkle, or any such thing, but that it should be holy and without blemish."

I am profoundly concerned that many believers in our current culture have lost their passion for purity and the honesty of holiness precisely because they have no sense that the King's return is truly imminent.

Would compromise with the world be so rampant in the church if we really believed Jesus was standing on our threshold with His nail-scarred hand raised in preparation to knock? Would Christians be so casual about, disrespectful toward, and dishonoring of the precious, time-honored things of God if they were ever mindful of the truth that He may split the eastern sky at their very next breath? Would we be so timid about sharing the love and message of the living Christ with our hell-bound neighbors and coworkers? Would we be more mindful of the fact that eternity is long and that heaven and hell are literal realities? Would we continue to be so painfully concerned about offending the delicate sensibilities of a dying culture or seeming politically incorrect?

What if we knew beyond all doubt that before sunrise tomorrow the graves of the righteous dead all over planet earth would burst open and that right behind them every sanctified, watching believer would be snatched away in an instant for a glorious meeting with our Savior in the sky? Would that knowledge modify our conversations? Would it reorder our priorities? Would it energize, animate, and inform our prayers?

I am utterly and absolutely convinced that at this moment we are indeed standing on the edge of the greatest event to transpire in human history since Jesus conquered death and hell in our stead and on our behalf through His sacrificial, atoning death and resurrection. The critical question each and every believer must get gut-level honest about and ask is, am I ready?

The betrothed Israelite bride I introduced you to in the prologue of this book kept her garments spotless as she eagerly awaited her sudden "abduction." In accordance with tradition that stealthy catching away was set into motion when the father gave the signal that all preparations were complete and the time was right. Then, and only then, could the bridegroom assemble the wedding party and begin the march from the father's house to the home of the bride. This took place most commonly around midnight.

As the boisterous procession moved along, the friends and family of the bridegroom would shout, "Behold, the bridegroom cometh! Behold, the bridegroom cometh!" At the head of this joyful parade marched a close friend blowing a *shofar*, or trumpet.

With this and everything else you have seen on the preceding pages in mind, read now with fresh eyes in its entirety this parable Jesus told His disciples concerning His coming:

> Then the kingdom of heaven shall be like ten virgins, who took their lamps and went out to meet the bridegroom. Five of them were wise and five were foolish. Those who were foolish took their lamps, but took no oil with them.

But the wise took jars of oil with their lamps. While the bridegroom delayed, they all rested and slept.

But at midnight there was a cry, "Look, the bridegroom is coming! Come out to meet him!"

Then all those virgins rose and trimmed their lamps. But the foolish said to the wise, "Give us some of your oil, for our lamps have gone out."

The wise answered, "No, lest there not be enough for us and you. Go rather to those who sell it, and buy some for yourselves."

But while they went to buy some, the bridegroom came, and those who were ready went in with him to the wedding banquet. And the door was shut.

Afterward, the other virgins came also, saying, "Lord, Lord, open the door for us."

But he answered, "Truly I say to you, I do not know you."

Watch therefore, for you know neither the day nor the hour in which the Son of Man is coming.

—MATTHEW 25:1–13

It is true. Only the Father knows the day and hour at which He will give that signal. But Jesus emphasized that we could know the *season*. And I am wholly convinced we are now in that extraordinary window of time in which the Father will look at the Son and, with a glorious glimmer in His eye, nod His approval. In that instant a jubilant wedding party will depart across the sapphire sill of heaven's gate on a direct heading for earth. When that multitudinous processional arrives, the Bridegroom will joyfully take what belongs to Him. He will abduct His bride.

The ancient Greeks had a word that well described such an event: *harpazo*. According to Strong's Concordance *harpazo* means "to seize; to carry off by force; or to snatch away."[4] This is precisely the word Paul used when encouraging the Thessalonians concerning the resurrection and the rapture:

"Then we who are alive and remain shall be *caught up* together with them in the clouds to meet the Lord in the air. And so we shall be forever with the Lord."[5]

What a thought! What a hope! Our righteous Redeemer, who purchased our salvation with the awful price of His own guiltless blood, will come to reclaim what by covenant belongs to Him and Him alone. He will not be denied, delayed, nor detoured! No government, no human institution, no devil nor demon, not even the law of gravity itself will be able to prevent us from that glorious meeting in the air.

It will not matter on that grand day if you are working two miles under the earth's surface in a coal mine or flying at five hundred miles per hour at forty thousand feet in a jet airliner. If you're blood-bought, you're coming out of here.

At salvage yards I have watched with fascination the operation of a giant crane with a mighty attached magnet. I have seen entire automobiles leap off the earth like a feather as the lever was thrown and power was supplied to that magnet. So will it be when the Savior of souls and champion of Calvary steps into the clouds. Oh, how we will leap from this cursed planet to the magnetic pull of His perfect person to meet Him in the air!

We will make our journey from here to that heavenly home and celestial city that our Bridegroom has been preparing just for us. There we will leap like young harts across the everlasting hills of God's glory in our eternal home—to suffer no more, sigh no more, cry no more, there to die no more.

In first century Israel the freshly "abducted" Jewish bride would be spirited away to her new home. Preparations for a lavish wedding feast would be under way, but first the couple would be sequestered in the wedding chamber for seven days. That's right; the couple would be hidden away, unseen, for a full week!

In the very same way the snatched-away church will be hidden away communing with Christ for a specific period of time before returning with Him to earth. How long? A *week* of years! That seven-year period will be filled with unspeakable bliss for those of us who are caught away to God's heaven. For those left behind on earth, those seven years will be a very different kind of experience.

As the redeemed enter the gates of that fair city on high, those left behind on this planet will experience the most cataclysmic, paradigm-shattering realization ever to explode upon the human consciousness.

My friend, you don't want to miss the appearance of the Bridegroom. You want to be "rapture ready." Are you? Your Bible says two will be grinding at the mill. One will be taken, and one will be left. A husband and wife will be asleep in the bed. He will be awakened by a soft rustling of the linens, reach across the bed, and find the other side vacated. He'll walk through the house and check for his wife and children. He will not find them.

Hundreds of millions will be gone in a moment, in the twinkling of an eye. Let me plead with you: don't miss that day. I fervently pray that you'll join me on "the first load out." Even so, I am aware that not every person will heed these warnings. I am also aware that you may have picked up this book *after* this extraordinary event has already transpired. That is why the next chapter will serve as your guide to what you can expect and, more importantly, what to *do* in the tragic event that you miss the rapture.

CHAPTER 7

How to Catch Up After the Church Has Been Caught Up

The Christian who prepares for the coming of the Lord may be scorned by all who say, "Peace and safety!" He will be eyed as a curiosity by those who, like people of Noah's day, know not until the flood comes. But when God splits the skies and the stars fall and men cry for the rocks and mountains, that will be his day![1]

—VANCE HAVNER (1901–1986)

ROUGHLY TWELVE MILES southeast of the center of Columbus, Ohio, you will find the sprawling campus of the church it has been my profound privilege to pastor for four decades. World Harvest Church, with more than half a million square feet under a single roof, rises up from the surrounding fertile, green fields at 4595 Gender Road. I want to be very sure all who need to find it can do so. Here are the precise GPS satellite coordinates: 39.8913, -82.8280.

On the north side of the campus, just outside Breakthrough Ministries' headquarters, you will find a small garden. At the center of that garden stands a white cross. Pointing skyward, it reminds all who see it of the direction every sanctified believer will be heading when that archangel shouts, "The Bridegroom cometh!" We're going up!

I bring this specific landmark to your attention because the answers to life's most pressing questions have always been found at the foot of the cross. That will literally be the case for those who find themselves left here on earth following the rapture of the saints not too many days from now. I have made sure of that.

Some time ago I commissioned skilled workmen to create a compartment within the concrete at the base of that cross for a very specific purpose. I have placed something there. The components of the contents of that hidden chamber are currently worth only a few dollars. However, a day is coming in which the truths contained therein will be priceless.

Within that void are written transcripts, video discs, and computer files all containing a message I preached several years ago providing specific instructions about what to do upon discovering the rapture has occurred. This is neither a joke nor some sort of publicity stunt. This is a life-and-death serious attempt to serve others and impact eternal destinies. I have spent my life pointing lost sinners to the saving grace of Jesus, and I plan to do so even after I'm gone.

I know that the days immediately following the instantaneous catching away of hundreds of millions of blood-washed believers around the world are going to be the most terrifying and panic-filled hours the earth's population has ever experienced. I also know that many of those who remain will know precisely what happened, no matter what lies the news media dreams to churn out.

You see, millions of unbelievers have been raised in Christian homes and had years of exposure to the truth about the last days. Countless others will have had a believing spouse or a born-again neighbor or even coworker who repeatedly testified to them about the end times and the imminent catching away of the church. When every committed Christian in their acquaintance instantly turns up missing amid an unprecedented global catastrophe, a horrifying truth will crash in upon their reeling consciousness: *it was all true.*

Everything they had been warned about and cavalierly

dismissed as religious scaremongering will be reality. Every word that Bible-believing, prophetic preaching Pastor Rod Parsley said will have unfolded just as he said it would.

For the doubters, the mockers, the scoffers, and the skeptics, the searing truth will dawn like a thousand suns. They will have been left behind. And I know precisely what their first impulse is going to be.

I will never forget our first church service following September 11, 2001. The attacks on America occurred on a Tuesday, and the next night we set a record for Wednesday service attendance. Rarely has World Harvest Church been so full on a weeknight unless we were hosting some sort of national conference. The same was true the following Sunday. We had extra chairs in the aisles and across the auditorium, and every overflow room was brimming with stunned, heartsick people looking for comfort and answers. Many of these were not regular church attenders. Some hadn't darkened our door in years. Yet in the midst of shock and disorienting grief their first impulse was to seek solace and meaning in the house of God.

I would never attempt to minimize anything that happened on that infamous day, nor dismiss the grievous losses suffered by so many. Nevertheless, *four* commercial airliners and *three* buildings were involved in that day's death, destruction, and sorrow. Please challenge your imagination for a moment. Stretch it to the breaking point to comprehend the global confusion, panic, and terror that will ensue in the hours and days immediately following the sudden, simultaneous disappearance of hundreds of millions around the world.

Scores, perhaps hundreds, of airliners fall from the sky, many of them striking population centers as they do. Runaway trains in every metropolitan area become projectiles. Within minutes the freeway systems of the world become little more than smoking, tangled webs of twisted metal and broken bodies as gridlock paralyzes the world's major cities. Looting, rioting, and violent lawlessness instantly surge as the basest of human desires and instances of every society and culture run amuck—sensing their opportunity to wreak havoc and seizing it.

Take the shock and terror of 9/11, the devastation wrought by the tsunamis that swept across Indonesia in 2004 and Japan in 2011, and the carnage of the 7.0-magnitude earthquake that leveled much of Haiti in 2010 and killed more than a quarter of a million people.[2] Roll all these woes together, and distribute their fury on a global scale, and you will still not have an inkling as to what the hours after the rapture of the church will be like for those left behind.

Hospital maternity wards will echo with the shrieks of mothers whose newborn infants vanished from their arms. Nurses will run the halls in panic as they process the reality that every last infant in their care has disappeared. In every hospital crib a tiny, plastic wristband offers silent testimony that only moments earlier a precious baby boy or girl had been there. Panicky text messages and phone calls by the tens of millions will go unanswered.

Yes, in the days following 9/11 our nation's church houses were full. But on the day after the abduction of the bride of Christ the panicked mobs will not wait for a regularly scheduled service. Those with enough knowledge of the Bible to comprehend what has really happened will storm the churches that preached the unadulterated Word of God. They will tear the doors off their hinges and climb over one another in hopes of finding some sort of loophole or reprieve.

Having experienced only a few hours of what earth is like without the restraining influence of the Holy Spirit and the preservative "salt" of His church, throngs of frightened, despairing people will fill churches like mine in hopes of finding an answer to the most urgent question they have ever faced:

What do I do now?

That is why I have placed that message—in every available medium—within the base of the cross. There actually *is* an answer to that question. A hopeful answer, in fact. I will share it with you too.

When I was a boy of about eight years of age, my family of four lived in a tiny two-bedroom apartment on the south side of Columbus, Ohio. This, by the way, was not the side of town where all the bankers, lawyers, and country club members lived. My sister and I shared a room with bunk beds, where I occupied the upper berth.

Many years later I will look back on this setting through adult eyes and realize those were spartan conditions for raising a young family. Yet my future recollections of this time will be of a happy home, rich with an abundance of love and faith and unity. However, on that night I had a terrifying experience that forever marked my soul.

I woke up from a deep sleep with a sense that something was wrong. Perhaps an unremembered dream troubled my spirit. Whatever the reason, I gingerly climbed down the bed so as not to awaken my sister, sleeping soundly in her bunk beneath me. I headed for my parents' bedroom seeking reassurance and comfort. I found their bedroom empty, the bed unmade, and their pajamas loosely laid out.

Having recently heard a sermon concerning the rapture of the church, my mind instantly leapt to a terrifying conclusion. *Jesus had caught His church away to heaven, and I had been left behind!* Panic rising in my heart, I ran through the other rooms of our little apartment searching for them. There was no sign of them anywhere. I was almost certain that my parents—the two most righteous, God-loving, Scripture-quoting people I knew—had been escorted off to heaven, while I was not found worthy. My sister and I were left behind and were on our own to fend for ourselves under the iron-fisted rule of the Antichrist.

Under the weight of this terrifying thought I burst into tears and began to sob. A moment later I heard muffled voices coming from the direction of our back door. I ran to it and threw it open to find my parents sitting on the back porch, looking at the stars and enjoying a casual conversation.

Now the tears streaming down my young cheeks were of relief, not despair. Through my sobs I told them what I thought had happened. Their response was exactly the right one for this moment. My mother said, "Son, do you want to pray? We'll make an altar right here and pray with you." I did. And we did.

My wise parents knew that nothing reassures the believer's heart like approaching the throne of grace for help in time of need. As I learned that night, the knowledge that you are right with God is a powerful, irreplaceable comfort.

So I must pause and ask you, are you really rapture ready? As I ask, I am somberly mindful of Jesus's words of caution against presumption:

> Not everyone who says to Me, "Lord, Lord," shall enter the kingdom of heaven, but he who does the will of My Father who is in heaven. Many will say to Me on that day, "Lord, Lord, have we not prophesied in Your name, cast out demons in Your name, and done many wonderful works in Your name?" But then I will declare to them, "I never knew you. Depart from Me, you who practice evil."
> —MATTHEW 7:21–23

It grieves me to know that many people who claim a casual affiliation with Christ are not truly rapture ready. These are first among those who will need to know what to do when the despair that I briefly felt as an eight-year-old boy becomes a daily reality. It is to them that I address the remainder of this chapter.

You have missed the catching away of the church but managed to survive the initial wave of death and destruction that claimed the lives of millions worldwide. Now what?

The first and most important thing you need to know is that there is still hope for your eternal soul. Yes, life in the tribulation period will be unspeakably hard, but it is only seven years long. Eternity is an unimaginably long time. The choices you make in the days and weeks ahead can secure your eternal future in heaven, even though they may cost you your life on earth. That is a trade every wise person will gladly make.

How do I know that individuals can still be saved after the catching away of the church? Because in the sixth and seventh chapters of Revelation—in the middle of the section of John's prophecy describing the horrific events of the tribulation period—we see people standing before the throne of God who have been martyred for the faith in this season of time:

> When He opened the fifth seal, I saw under the altar the souls of those who had been slain for the word of God and for the testimony they had held. They cried out with a loud voice, "How long, O Sovereign Lord, holy and true, until You judge and avenge our blood on those who dwell on the earth?" Then a white robe was given to each of them, and they were told to rest a little longer, until the number of their fellow servants and brothers should be completed, who would be killed as they were.
> —Revelation 6:9–11

The following chapter confirms that this white-robed throng comprises people born again during the tribulation period. John sees this group, and then one of the twenty-four elders queries John about them:

"Who are these clothed in white robes, and where did they come from?"

I said to him, "Sir, you know."

He said to me, "*These are those who came out of great tribulation and washed their robes and made them white in the blood of the Lamb.* Therefore, they are before the throne of God, and serve Him day and night in His temple. And He who sits on the throne will dwell among them."

—REVELATION 7:13–15, EMPHASIS ADDED

Here is the good news: being left behind in the rapture does not mean there is no hope for eternal salvation. The power of the precious blood of Jesus to wash the vilest sinner clean is just as effective now as it was before the catching away of the church. There is still hope for you.

Here is the bad news: taking a stand for Jesus is going to require more resolve, courage, and fortitude than at any other time in Christian history. You are about to be faced with unprecedented global upheaval combined with a fierce, systematic persecution.

You must heed the warnings I am about to give you. At the instant of the rapture, a seven-year countdown clock began ticking. In heaven a book of judgment that has been sealed with a sevenfold seal since the foundation of the world is about to be opened.

I know you think things are bad now, but I must be frank with you. They are going to get much, much worse. For a short season Satan will control entire portions of planet earth. Nevertheless, try not to panic. It has never been more important to make sound decisions.

Next are seven key instructions to follow. They will increase your chances of surviving in the days ahead, but much more importantly they will ensure that you don't miss the final opportunity to inherit eternal life before the door to heaven closes for all time.

1. Don't believe the lies of the media.

If you think the media has been biased and agenda-driven before today, just wait until the world is dying, the moon is bleeding, and the seas are seething under the whiplash of fury as they spill their dead into the lap of God.

In the aftermath of the rapture it will be very important to the satanically inspired global authorities that the masses not know the truth about the disappearance of hundreds of millions of people worldwide. They will not want you to embrace the obvious conclusion that the Bible was right and that Jesus is precisely who He said He was. That will require them to come up with a plausible alternative explanation.

My best guess is that you are already being told that an extraterrestrial invasion is responsible for the mass disappearances. Such a thesis might have seemed ludicrous a week prior to the rapture. But with hundreds of millions missing and millions more dead and dying, anything now seems plausible. Several decades of science fiction movies about alien invasions have served as excellent preconditioning for believing this fabrication. Responding to this threat will be the justification for imposing unprecedented levels of control over society and draconian curbs on individual freedoms.

A global government is emerging in response to this global crisis. The measures of control the members of this government will propose will seem quite reasonable given the scale of the challenges facing mankind. But do not believe what they say. Behind the benevolent language and rational-sounding demands lies a demonic trap from which there is no exit.

2. Repent and accept Jesus Christ as Savior.

This is the most important item on this list. I have listed it second only because if you don't heed the first item—that is, ignoring the lies of the media—you might not heed this one.

Even in this temporary season of evil's reign upon the earth one blessed truth has not been repealed: "Whosoever shall call upon the name of the Lord shall be saved."[3] The sincere, repentant heart still finds mercy and cleansing at the foot of the cross. "There is a fountain filled with blood drawn from Emmanuel's veins; and sinners plunged beneath that flood lose all their guilty stains."[4]

The Father still stands vigil on His porch, scanning the horizon for the growing speck that represents a returning prodigal son or daughter. He still casts His tunic aside and runs to meet every wayward child who comes home, throwing His arms around each and putting His signet ring upon that child's mud-stained, trembling fingers.

Even now, as deep darkness descends upon the world, when all that is pure and good and sweet has been withdrawn into heaven for a season, even now you can pray this prayer and become a child of God:

> *Heavenly Father, I rejected Jesus. I waited one day too long, but I pray now, God, have mercy on my soul. Forgive my sins! Wash me in Your blood! Preserve me! Help me through this time! I want to go to heaven!*

3. Bring your loved ones to heaven with you (if you can).

Of course, once you've prayed that prayer, you're going to want to reach every family member and loved one you can with the truth. Encourage everyone you can to receive Christ, but those who won't listen will have to be avoided going forward. A powerful spirit of deception—the Bible calls it a "strong delusion"[5]—will be sweeping the earth unhindered and unrestrained, so you must move quickly. When the Antichrist emerges and starts demanding universal worship and allegiance, you won't be able to trust anyone.

Be careful to whom you speak. Be careful what you say. The authorities will soon be hunting down believers like rabid dogs.

4. Secure your access to the Word of God.

Find all the Bibles you can get your hands on, and hide them in a variety of secure places. Very soon they're going to be confiscating them. Those blessed words of life are going to be viewed as a dangerous, seditious threat to the peace and stability of the satanic global order. Possession of a Bible will be a capital crime.

They're going to take all the Bibles they can find, throw them in a giant pile, and set them ablaze. They'll dance around that bonfire with unbridled glee as the only remaining source of truth on planet earth is reduced to cinders and ashes. Electronic versions of the Scriptures will be forbidden as well, although much harder to find and destroy.

Perhaps you couldn't make time to read God's Word back when it wasn't a crime to do so. But as any Christian survivor of the Soviet Empire will testify, you'll treasure it here in a day in which merely possessing it can cost you everything. You'll need that eternal truth too—not only as a source of strength, but also as a guide. I recommend that you start with the Book of Revelation because it will reveal and explain the events through which you're about to live.

You will also want to read the Book of Daniel. Ezekiel too, particularly chapters 38 and 39. Read the twenty-first chapter of Luke and Matthew chapter 24. Get the Word of God in you. Memorize it.

5. Make no alliance with the Antichrist.

This is vitally important. Indeed, it is not hyperbole to say it is a matter of eternal life and death.

Do you recall my description, back in the first chapter, of the first century cult of emperor worship? Every individual living within the vast Roman Empire was required to acknowledge the lordship of Caesar by burning an incense offering at one of the many temples scattered throughout the domain and swearing an oath of allegiance. Those who refused were

arrested and executed, were enslaved, or became fugitive out-
casts, unable to participate in Roman society or commerce.

As the lights go out all over the world and spiritual darkness
envelops every culture and society, something similar will grip
the world by the throat. This will be much worse and far more
effective than any previous regime because it will be enabled
and enforced by the latest technologies.

You must swear no allegiance to any one-world leader. Make
no compromise with the one-world religious system. Above all
else, do not take any identifying mark or implant, no matter
how reasonable the explanations or justifications to do so may
sound. This new system of identification will be mandatory for
anyone participating in the financial system at any level, or to
qualify to receive government food aid amid global famine and
mass starvation.

I will repeat this vital warning. Pledge no allegiance to the
new one-world system or its leader. Accept no identifying mark
or implant required to participate in the new economic system.

6. Prepare to become a survivalist.

If you follow my counsel in the previous point, and I pray for
the sake of your eternal soul that you do, then you're going to
have a big problem on your hands. You will not be allowed to
have a job, hold a bank account, or participate in the economy
in any way. In fact, you will most likely become a wanted fugitive, hunted by the hell-inspired authorities as by a pack of ravenous wolves.

That means you're going to have to find a way to survive "off
the grid" and in the wild, much as our pioneer ancestors did.
You'll need to move as far away from urban centers as possible. Your objective is to survive for seven years. If you can
do that, you are home free. But doing so will mean learning
to kill or scavenge what you eat. Shelter from the elements,
water, and food will be your primary challenges, complicated

by the need to remain out of the eye of a powerful, high-tech "surveillance state."

Any skills or gear conducive to living the life of a stone age hunter-gatherer will serve you well. Just make sure you have removed any RFID tags in anything you take with you. These increasingly ubiquitous computer chips are likely to be exploited by the authorities for tracking purposes.

7. Prepare to suffer and even die for your faith.

The chances of avoiding capture for seven long years are not good. What's more, as a blood-washed Jesus follower in a world system largely under Satan's influence you will be hated with an unimaginable hatred by the Antichrist's systems of control.

Once again the horrors suffered by the Christian martyrs of the first century at the hands of the demonic Roman emperors provide a reliable guide as to what to expect if you are captured. For a more recent reminder of what happens when Satan's cruelty is given free expression through demonized men, look to the genocidal atrocities of ISIS in Syria and Iraq. There, in the name of Allah and accompanied by citations from the Quran, the most unspeakable tortures are visited daily upon Christians, Yazidis, and Kurds. These men, in the name of their religion, combine human creativity with hell's darkest and most sadistic hatreds to come up with new and ever-more inventive ways to publicly torture and kill. The objective is to instill abject fear and complete submission in others.

The same will be true, but magnified, in the Antichrist system. Satan does not want casualties; he wants converts. He wants people to worship the image of the Beast created by the False Prophet. Satan has always craved man's worship.

You must be strong and resolute in the face of these horrors. Do not take the mark, even in the face of torture for yourself or your loved ones. For inspiration, read *Foxe's Book of Martyrs*. In it you will find many stories of believers who chose painful deaths rather than renouncing Christ. This is a choice you may face as well. A few hours of pain to gain eternity in heaven and avoid an everlasting hell is an exchange well worth making.

If you are reading this prior to the catching away of the church, then there is still time to avoid everything I've just described. If you have not done so already, give your life to Jesus today. Don't miss the rapture!

Don't be deceived. There is no neutral ground here. If you will not be marked for Christ now, you will be marked for Antichrist then. You will be branded as a rancher brands his cattle.

So I ask, one more time, are you rapture ready? "For in an hour you least expect, the Son of Man is coming!"[6] Any day now the magnificent magnitude of His perfect person is going to sweep out from north to south, and from east to west to catch His people away. If you are blood-washed and looking for His coming, you will be among that blessed number.

CHAPTER 8

The Lion-Lamb of God

*Our Lord Jesus will certainly bring to nought all the opposition
made to his kingdom, and bring to ruin all those who make
that opposition and persist in it. He will be too hard for those,
whoever they may be, that fight against Him, against His
subjects, and the interests of his kingdom among men.*[1]

—MATTHEW HENRY (1662–1714)

LET US NOW return to John's narrative of his extraordinary
Patmos vision. When we last saw the beloved disciple in
chapter 4 of Revelation, he had been caught up into heaven and
glimpsed the throne room of the great I Am Himself. There,
extraordinary "living creatures," twenty-four elders, and a vast
crystal sea of saints all participate in the greatest worship service ever taken in by mortal eyes.

Chapter 5 opens with a new development. John notices a
scroll in God's right hand. This scroll is covered front and back
with writing, but it is sealed with seven seals. A "strong angel"
asks, "Who is worthy to open the scroll and to break its seals?"[2]
The answer to that question is a stunning divine paradox. Just
as John is about to despair of anyone worthy being found, one
of the twenty-four elders shouts, "Look! The Lion of the tribe
of Judah, the Root of David, has triumphed. He is able to open
the scroll and to loose its seven seals."[3] But when John looks,
he sees not a lion but a lamb, "standing as though it had been
slain."[4] In other words, the worthy One is a triumphant Lion

who appears to be a slaughtered Lamb. This, of course, is the risen Savior, Jesus. Notice that Jesus is seen "standing." He is standing, rather than sitting, because He just got back from meeting His bride in the air and escorting her back to the wedding chamber. He has not yet had time to take His seat of honor and dominion at the right hand of the Father.

Over the following six chapters the Lion-Lamb of God will progressively open those seals, each one triggering an event on earth designed to lead toward the ultimate defeat of the Antichrist and the destruction of his satanic system.

FOUR HORSEMEN

The first four seals result in the progressive release of what are commonly referred to as "the four horsemen of the apocalypse." These four riders, each on a horse of a differing color, are the Antichrist, War, Famine, and Death. They ride horses of white, red, black, and pale, respectively.

In the past some interpreters have suggested the rider of the white horse who goes forth to conquer is Christ Himself. This is primarily because we do see Jesus on a white horse later in John's vision. This is an incorrect assumption, however.

Christ is *already* victorious. In fact, in the previous chapter Jesus, the Lion-Lamb, is declared to already have triumphed. He has nothing left to conquer. No. Here the rider of the white horse represents the world leader who will eventually be revealed to be the Antichrist, who will attempt to conquer but ultimately fail. How do I know this rider is the Antichrist? A clue is embedded in John's description of this rider:

> And I looked, and there before me was a white horse. He who sat on it had a bow. And a crown was given to him, and he went forth conquering that he might overcome.
> —REVELATION 6:2

Do you see it? This rider has a bow, but he has no arrows! I've rarely seen a more apt image of the devil. His primary power derives from invoking fear and through deception. Of course, we live in a generation that has forgotten how to tell the good guys from the bad guys. Thus, the Antichrist slips onto a white horse in order to gain power by deceiving the gullible.

He promises peace but has no intention of providing it. In fact, his rule is characterized by war. He says he will be a beneficent provider, but his real agenda is to become a ruthless dictator. He claims his administration will be accompanied by acceptance and tolerance, but the only ones accepted and tolerated in his regime are those who will give him absolute and unquestioning allegiance. It is true he has a crown, symbolizing authority, but it was given to him by the Dragon, Satan—and by men who are deceived by his flattery and false promises.

Even so, for the first three and a half years of the tribulation period the Antichrist does not show his true colors. He appears to most of the world to be a gifted, charismatic leader doing his best to help the world regain stability and peace in the midst of a global crisis of unprecedented proportions. As his profile rises, his power and influence grow.

Very early in the first half of the tribulation period his reputation as a peacemaker will soar when he brokers a peace deal in the Middle East that not only solves the seemingly unsolvable conflict between Israel and her Arab neighbors but also paves the way for the construction of the third temple in Jerusalem.

Of course, it will take a diplomat such as the world has never seen to resolve an issue so intractable. Any statesman who finds a way to bring peace between the descendants of Ishmael and the sons of Isaac will possess the patience of Job, the wisdom of Solomon, the wealth of Midas, the analytic genius of Einstein, and the iron will of Churchill. The person who resolves the bitter and long-standing feud between Muslims and Jews—who can remove this excruciating thorn in the side of the world—will be hailed a leader with no equal. And he will be. As the Book of Daniel reveals, the deal the Antichrist will broker is built upon a peace treaty between the government he leads and the government of Israel. I will revisit this point in a later chapter.

The opening of three more seals follows. These result in three additional horsemen riding forth, bringing war, famine, and death to significant portions of the world. Please note that I said "portions" of the world. Contrary to popular understanding, the Antichrist never successfully establishes control of the whole planet. Refuges, sanctuaries, and entire nations outside his dominion remain throughout the tribulation period. However, due to the increasing interdependence of nations, a global economy, and nearly instantaneous means of communication, no place on earth will be entirely immune to his influence.

It's no coincidence that the second of these horses is red—the color of blood. From the blood of the righteous Abel to the blood of the latest victims of sectarian violence the world over, the earth has been soaked in scarlet blood. An immeasurable quantity of blood has been shed by the purges of Stalin's Russia and Mao's China, the killing fields of Cambodia, and the genocides and atrocities that have taken place more recently. But all of these combined will be nothing more than crimson footnotes compared with the violence that will visit the earth when the red horse rider goes forth to accomplish his bloodthirsty mission.

According to some estimates the world's population will grow to about 9.7 billion by the year 2050. No one can venture to guess how many multiplied millions will die violently as War swings his cruel sword during the dark days of the tribulation.

But as gruesome as War is, he has a close friend who is perhaps even more lethal. The opening of the third seal releases another horror that is never far from the previous one: a black horse rider known as Famine. His purpose is to restrict the food supply. Famine will cause people to give all they have in order to procure just enough food to sustain their lives.

Famine accompanies war because war often makes the means of producing food impossible. Not only do advancing armies strip a country of any food it has, but also war destroys all means of food production, cutting survivors off from the possibility of sustaining themselves.

War not only disrupts the means of producing food but also displaces people escaping the violence of conflict, making sowing and reaping impossible. Those who are on the run or living in refugee camps have neither the time nor the means to sow seed or harvest a crop. As a result, they must depend on aid from others to survive. War and Famine together present a double-barreled dilemma for multitudes.

But the trouble is still not finished. The opening of the fourth seal reveals a two-for-one special: a pale horse—the color of a corpse—carrying two ghastly riders, Death and Hades. These horsemen come to claim the millions that will be their unwilling victims. These four riders traverse the earth throughout the tribulation period, bringing untold grief and destruction to every place that is scheduled on their unholy itinerary.

A HEAVENLY LAWSUIT

For the first half of the tribulation period it may appear that the Antichrist and his allies are actually getting away with their grandiose plans and machinations. Countless tribulation saints lose their lives standing strong for their newfound faith, with seemingly no consequences for the perpetrators. Thus, the opening of the fifth seal results not in an event on earth but in a discussion in the court of heaven:

> When He opened the fifth seal, I saw under the altar the souls of those who had been slain for the word of God and for the testimony they had held. They cried out with

a loud voice, "How long, O Sovereign Lord, holy and
true, until You judge and avenge our blood on those who
dwell on the earth?" Then a white robe was given to each
of them, and they were told to rest a little longer, until
the number of their fellow servants and brothers should
be completed, who would be killed as they were.

—REVELATION 6:9–11

I mentioned this passage previously as evidence that people
will still be born again on earth even after the catching away
of the church. At the breaking of the fifth seal we hear the
cries of those saints who have already been executed for their
faith during the tribulation period. The imagery and language
here is reminiscent of a legal courtroom in which complain-
ants come before a judge seeking justice for wrongs done to
them. The judge hears their complaint and instructs them to
be patient and to "rest a little longer." Justice against Satan and
his willing human pawns is coming soon. The cup of his guilt
for murdering God's people has not yet been filled to the brim.

Even so, the tribulation saints don't have to wait long. The
breaking of the very next seal will begin a full-scale assault on
Antichrist's would-be empire before he's even had a chance to
reveal himself and take his unholy throne.

"THE GREAT DAY OF HIS WRATH"

The opening of the sixth seal results in an earthquake of
unprecedented scale. In Revelation 6:12–14 the Word of God
uses extraordinarily vivid language to describe the worldwide
effects of this tectonic event, which may include the eruption
of hundreds of volcanoes spewing ash skyward and darkening
the skies. John writes of the sun turning as black as sackcloth,
the moon turning to blood, the stars being obliterated, and the
heavens receding like a rolled-up scroll. He describes an earthquake so intense that "every mountain and island was removed
from its place."[5]

In Matthew 24:29 Jesus, quoting the prophet Joel,[6] prophetically described this same event when He warned the disciples: "Immediately after the tribulation of those days, 'the sun will be darkened, the moon will not give its light; the stars will fall from heaven, and the powers of the heavens will be shaken.'"

Equally sobering is John's description of the effects of this earthquake on humanity:

> Then the kings of the earth and the great men and the rich men and the commanding officers and the strong and everyone, slave and free, hid themselves in the caves and in the rocks of the mountains. They said to the mountains and rocks, "Fall on us, and hide us from the face of Him who sits on the throne, and from the wrath of the Lamb, for the great day of His wrath has come. Who is able to withstand it?"
>
> —Revelation 6:15–17

Yes, with the breaking of the sixth seal, everything escalates as together nature and nature's God essentially declare war on the Antichrist.

It's important to understand that God is fully in control here. He works throughout the seven-year tribulation period to accomplish His predetermined ends, particularly concerning the salvation of Israel and the Jewish people. The Antichrist dreams of asserting total control, but he is never allowed to fully gain his footing.

The ultimate objective of the cataclysmic events unleashed by the breaking of these seven seals is the defeat of the Antichrist. This is news to many believers who have been taught all their lives that the tribulation period was a time of God's raining down wrath and vengeance upon those who rejected His Son.

God loves people with a tenacious, relentless love. His activities throughout history have always and only had mankind's redemption as their goal. God's every act and intervention on the world stage have sought to legally reverse the curse inflicted upon the world through Adam's rebellion.

Of course, that tragic insurrection was masterminded by a great deceiver. Here in this season of travail God's ancient enemy is being dealt with once and for all time. A holy God is not about to allow the Antichrist, his False Prophet, or his hell-spawned Beast system to have their way. So the hammer blows from heaven will begin to fall in earnest with the breaking of the seventh seal.

Before that seal is removed, however, John's perspective momentarily moves from earthquake-ravaged earth back to heaven. Revelation chapter 7 represents a pause in what has up to this point been the rapid-fire breaking of the seals. In this interlude the beloved disciple witnesses something quite extraordinary.

144,000 WITNESSES

Allow me to remind you that the Antichrist does not fully reveal himself until the midpoint of the tribulation period. It is at this juncture that we move into the three-and-one-half-year season known as the great tribulation. Prior to this transition the would-be "god" appears merely to be a benevolent world leader rising in prominence and power. He is that rider on a white horse riding forth to conquer, but his conquests take the form of increasing influence and prestige on the world stage and expanding authority over the bureaucracies of global government. He is viewed as a champion for peace, bringing reconciliation among the warring regional, ethnic, and religious blocs of planet earth.

Then, just as he drops the mask and reveals himself to be the malignant despot he truly is, something remarkable takes place right under his nose:

> And I saw another angel ascending from the east, having the seal of the living God. He cried out with a loud voice to the four angels who had been given power to harm the earth and the sea, saying, "Do not harm the earth or the sea or the trees, until we have sealed the servants of our God on their foreheads." Then I heard the number of those who were sealed, *one hundred and forty-four thousand out of every tribe of the children of Israel.*
> —REVELATION 7:2–4, EMPHASIS ADDED

Even at the pinnacle of his power and influence Satan and his proxy-puppet, the Antichrist, find themselves impotent to stop God from calling and sealing an army of anointed gospel ministers from among the twelve tribes of Israel. Twelve-thousand Holy Ghost–filled preachers from each Israelite tribe, totaling 144,000, fan out across the world to proclaim the gospel with power and bring in a final harvest of souls.

This army will lead the greatest revival that the world has ever known and will do so at the very moment Satan's hollow boasts and threats are the loudest and most grandiose.

Just writing these words makes me want to shout and dance for joy at the sheer awesomeness of our God. Even after the church is withdrawn, God is still in control. With no one left on earth to preach, God sends an angel to declare the gospel, and 144,000 respond. They, in turn, go forth and win souls out of every nation, kindred, tribe, and tongue.

We see this army of "sealed" Jewish evangelists again in the fourteenth chapter of Revelation. There they are declared to be a "first fruits" offering of the final worldwide harvest of souls: "These are those who follow the Lamb wherever He goes. These were redeemed from among men, as first fruits to God and to the Lamb. No lie was found in their mouths, for they are without fault before the throne of God."[7]

Let this sink in. Even when the church is gone and the

Antichrist is trying to run things, God has a revival. I don't know about you, but that just blesses me.

Even so, the worst is yet to come for the man of sin and those who follow him. With the breaking of the seventh and final seal, the once-and-for-all defeat of the rebellion birthed in deception and betrayal in the Garden of Eden begins in earnest.

CHAPTER 9

Decoding the Antichrist

*The tribulation period will witness the wrath of Satan in his
animosity against Israel...and of Satan's puppet, the Beast, in his
animosity against the saints....Yet even this manifestation of wrath
does not begin to exhaust the outpouring of wrath of that day.*[1]

—J. Dwight Pentecost (1915–2014)

In Revelation chapter 8 John's narrative returns to the breaking of the last of the seven scroll seals. At this moment we are essentially midway through the seven-year tribulation period. The remaining three-and-a-half-year stretch is known as the great tribulation. As the name suggests, the magnitude of everything in this second half increases dramatically.

Here the Antichrist drops the mask, revealing himself to be an aspiring world dictator with a ravenous craving to be worshipped as a god, after the pattern of the Roman emperor Nero in the first century. What's more, by overlaying parallel prophetic passages from Daniel and Ezekiel, and the words of Jesus Himself, we can deduce that at this point the Antichrist breaks his covenant with the nation of Israel and, in a betrayal for the ages, makes war with her instead, setting up his kingdom in the holy city of Jerusalem.

Ezekiel 38:11 indicates that during this time Israel is living at peace in cities and villages that are "unwalled"—that is, they have no need of defensive fortifications. I believe this will be possible due to the diplomatic skill of the man who will eventually be revealed as the Antichrist. He will make a covenant with Israel guaranteeing her safety and will arrange for Arabs and Jews to accommodate one another in a fashion never before seen. This peace deal will pave the way for him to be accepted as a world leader without peer.

Of course, this arrangement will not last beyond the midpoint of the tribulation. The Antichrist will demand worship and will go so far as to desecrate the temple as a sign that he is renouncing his covenant with Israel.

In a cryptic yet shockingly prescient passage recorded hundreds of years before its fulfillment Daniel 9:27 says, "He will confirm a covenant with many for one 'seven.' In the middle of the 'seven' he will put an end to sacrifice and offering. And at the temple he will set up an abomination that causes desolation, until the end that is decreed is poured out on him" (NIV). Something significant happens "in the middle of the 'seven'" (or three and a half years) that Daniel calls "an abomination that causes desolation." Perhaps this is an idolatrous image of the Antichrist himself erected as an object of worship. Whatever it is, its installation marks the point at which things go from very bad to very much worse.

Here is the warning that Jesus gave about this event: "So when you see the 'abomination of desolation,' spoken of by Daniel the prophet, standing in the holy place (let the reader understand), then let those who are in Judea flee to the mountains.... For then will be great tribulation, such as has not happened since the beginning of the world until now, no, nor ever shall be" (Matt. 24:15–16, 21).

As we're about to see, cracking open the seventh seal will result in the progressive sounding of seven trumpets, each successive blast triggering a catastrophic event on earth. However, before any trumpet sounds, the opening of the final seal first produces something extraordinary and quite ominous—utter quiet.

> When He opened the seventh seal, there was silence in
> heaven for about half an hour.
>
> —REVELATION 8:1

This is a stunning contrast to everything John has witnessed up to this point. The divine business he observed in the first seven chapters has been filled with sound. Heaven rings with loud, trumpet-like voices; the shouts of living creatures; the jubilant praise of innumerable throngs of worshippers; and thunderous proclamations. Not so in this moment. A holy hush settles over the court of heaven as the grimly serious business of permanently smashing the ages-old satanic rebellion enters its final phase.

God is about to unleash His wrath. Yet His anger is not aimed at the people He sent His Son to redeem, but rather upon the Antichrist and the vile kingdom he is attempting to set up. Nevertheless, the millions upon millions who have said a stubborn, hard-hearted "no" to history's final altar call, choosing to ally themselves with Satan instead, will find themselves caught up in this horrific outpouring of earth-purifying fire.

A seven-trumpet hurricane is brewing. This half-hour season of silence is the calm before that storm. Those trumpets unfold in Revelation chapters 8 through 11 as follows:

- **The first trumpet**—Ecological disaster. Hail and fire mixed with blood are thrown to the earth, burning up a third of the trees on the planet and all green grass.

- **The second trumpet**—A great burning mountain plunges into the sea, wiping out a third of all sea life. A third of all ocean-going vessels are destroyed, and a third of the seas turn a blood-like red.

Please keep in mind that these judgments are aimed at wrecking the Antichrist's system of global commerce. Heaven's wrath is thwarting the grand plans and schemes of this false messiah and would-be world ruler.

- **The third trumpet**—A "great star" called Wormwood falls to the earth, rendering a third of the planet's freshwater sources toxic and lethal.

- **The fourth trumpet**—The light emanating from the sun, moon, and stars is diminished by a third after these celestial bodies are "struck."

The final three trumpets produce three consecutive proclamations of "woe." Foreshadowing this threefold judgment, John sees an angel flying through the midst of heaven's realm, proclaiming: "Woe, woe, woe to the inhabitants of the earth, because of the other trumpet blasts of the three angels, who are yet to sound!" [2]

- **The fifth trumpet**—Here we have the first of the three "woe" judgments. At the sounding of the trumpet, a "star" falls from heaven to earth. Keep in mind that angelic beings are frequently symbolized by stars in prophetic language.

This star, or angel, is given the key to a bottomless pit. The unsealing of this pit releases smoke that temporarily blots out the sunlight. From out of the smoke a swarm of creatures is unleashed that in varying respects resemble some combination of locusts, horses, and scorpions. These terrifying creatures have a king named *Abaddon*, which means destroyer. They are unleashed upon the earth to torment, but not kill, any person who does not have the seal of God on his forehead.

By the way, many gifted expositors of Revelation have attempted to identify these creatures, which seem to be out of the realm of science fiction or some other genre beyond mortal knowledge. They may be exactly as John described them. On the other hand, they may be something that was so far out of his frame of reference that he could only attempt to explain them using terms that were familiar to him and his contemporaries. Let's afford John some grace in this matter. How do you describe something that has never been seen before—not just by you but also by any human?

Whatever they are, for five long months these swarms bring agonizing pain, without the relief of death, to unregenerate mankind by means of stings from their scorpion-like tails. The victims long for a death that does not come.

I know what it is like to attempt to comfort those who have experienced torment in this lifetime that would make dying look easy by comparison.

Think for a moment, if you dare, of the pain endured by a third-degree burn victim or someone who has had severe trauma due to a life-threatening accident. This is only an approximation of the agony that millions will feel from the attacks of these diabolical creatures. Their victims will seek death by any means, but despite their attempts to end the pain, death will escape them. And regardless of how bad their suffering is, and how desperate those who seek death become, this state of affairs lasts for only five months. It will seem like eternity but will be just a brief and comparatively mild foreshadowing of what eternity will be like separated from God. Woe, indeed.

When this horrifying season finally comes to a close, John offers a brief but bone-chilling commentary. He writes, "The first woe is past. Now, two more woes are yet to come."[3]

- **The sixth trumpet**—The second of the three "woes" involves the release of four fallen angels who have been bound at the Euphrates River since the fall of mankind, awaiting this very moment in time. Once liberated, they summon a

force of two hundred million mounted followers.
Before their work is done, they will kill a third
of the remaining human population via "plagues"
of fire, smoke, and brimstone.

We will reencounter this army, along with others from less exotic origins, in the next chapter. But for now let us focus on the fate of humanity. In the face of such horrors you would think that those who have followed after the Antichrist and willingly worshipped him might be reevaluating their choice of gods. But you would be wrong. As John informs us:

> The rest of mankind, who were not killed by these plagues, did not repent of the works of their hands. They did not cease to worship demons, and idols of gold, silver, brass, stone, and wood, which cannot see nor hear nor walk. Nor did they repent of their murders or their magical arts or their sexual immorality or their thefts.
>
> —REVELATION 9:20–21

How is this possible? How can people endure unspeakably harsh consequences and still not reconsider their ways? We see the very same thing all around us today. The horrific consequences of sin don't deter those it ravages. It is because sin blinds the eyes of the soul. It hardens the heart and sears the conscience. Sin darkens the mind and warps the will. As the nineteenth-century British preacher John Henry Jowett rightly said:

> Sin is a blasting presence, and every fine power shrinks and withers in the destructive heat. Every spiritual delicacy succumbs to its malignant touch.... Sin impairs the sight, and works towards blindness. Sin benumbs the hearing and tends to make men deaf. Sin perverts the taste, causing men to confound the sweet with the bitter,

and the bitter with the sweet. Sin hardens the touch, and eventually renders a man "past feeling." [4]

Before the sounding of the seventh and final trumpet John's narrative pauses once again. The tenth chapter is a vision concerning a "mighty angel" who presents John with a small open book and bids him to eat it.

Then the first half of chapter 11 pulls back and describes a series of events that take place in Jerusalem during the three-and-a-half-year run of the great tribulation. In other prophetic passages this very same time period is also enumerated as forty-two months, "time, times, and half a time," and 1,260 days. Here we meet the "two witnesses" who appear in Jerusalem, right in the Antichrist's new front yard, and begin declaring the Word of God. Throughout the great tribulation the minions of the Antichrist attempt to silence these preachers but are powerless to do so as long as the protection of God's anointing rests upon them:

> "And I will give power to my two witnesses, and they will prophesy for one thousand two hundred and sixty days, clothed in sackcloth." These are the two olive trees and the two candlesticks standing before the God of the earth. If anyone desires to harm them, fire proceeds out of their mouth and devours their enemies. If anyone desires to harm them, he must be killed in this way.
>
> —REVELATION 11:3–5

Countless expositors, many more learned than I, have attempted to solve the puzzle of the identities of these two mysterious witnesses. Popular candidates include Moses and Elijah, and Enoch and Elijah. I don't trouble myself with that question. For me it doesn't really matter. I'll be enjoying heaven when they appear, and I hope you'll be there too.

However, we'll come back to them later because they play a role in the final day of the tribulation period, which just happens to mark the first day of Christ's millennial reign. As we're about to see, that's when we'll be returning with our Canaan-conquering King. In fact, the seventh trumpet blast is followed by a pronouncement about that very day.

- **The seventh trumpet**—This is the final trumpet to sound and the final woe. Loud voices in heaven proclaim Christ's complete, everlasting victory. They declare, "The kingdoms of this world have become the kingdom of our Lord, and of His Christ, and He shall reign forever and ever."[5] The twenty-four elders fall on their faces, and a worship revival breaks out across heaven's vast domain. The temple of God that is before the throne is opened, accompanied by a great demonstration of God's awe-inspiring power—a prelude to a final outpouring of judgment upon the Antichrist and those who support him.

The most important thing that remains is for the King to return to earth to take His rightful place on the throne of David in Jerusalem. However, instead of continuing this chronology by immediately depicting Jesus's return to earth to claim the spoils of His victory, John's narrative doubles back and jumps around in time over the next eight chapters. Revelation chapters 12 through 19 represents a nonchronological view of the ages-long chess match between God and His weaker, foolish, hate-blinded adversary, Satan. For example, chapter 12 symbolically reveals a pivotal moment in that battle for the fate of the human race. John receives a behind-the-scenes look at the moment deity took on human flesh and dwelt among us.

He sees "a great sign" in the sky. It is a woman, great with child and in labor. Then another sign appears. A seven-headed dragon lurks near the woman with the aim of devouring her child as soon as he is born. Obviously this is no ordinary child about to be delivered:

> She gave birth to a male Child, "who was to rule all nations with an iron scepter." And her Child was caught up to God and to His throne.
>
> —REVELATION 12:5

You do not have to be a biblical scholar to discern what this sign in the heavens depicts. The woman is Israel. Through the millennia Satan repeatedly attempted to prevent the coming of the Messiah through the nation of Israel. Having failed to prevent His birth, Satan then repeatedly attempted to destroy that "child," but His resurrection and ascension thwarted the Dragon's plans for all time. All that was left to the Dragon was to vent his frustrated rage upon the woman—the nation of Israel.

This sign in the heavens actually exposes the spiritual roots of anti-Semitism—a dressed-up term for hatred of Jewish people. Here in these last days this ancient, hell-spawned animosity is spreading like a cancer across our world. Perhaps it is more accurate to say it is rising to the surface, for anti-Semitism has always been with us, lurking beneath the surface of virtually every culture in the world.

Why is this so? Many in our time point the accusing finger at the nation of Israel. They claim that this animosity springs from resentment over Israel's presence in the Middle East. Yet this explanation doesn't stand up to scrutiny. Long before Israel existed, Satan was fanning the flames of hatred against Jews.

No. The "Dragon" is enraged against the "woman" because she was God's chosen instrument for bringing the Savior into the world—the very One who brought about his utter defeat and humiliation. This is why a long list of despots and dictators—from Pharaoh to Herod to Nero to Hitler—have sought to wipe her out. All have failed. All have dashed themselves upon the rocks of God's Genesis promise to faithful Abraham and his offspring: "I will bless those who bless you, and curse those who curse you."[6]

In his vision of the woman, the Child, and the enraged Dragon in the heavens John glimpses a reenactment of a conflict the roots of which run back to the very Garden of Eden, where God prophesied to the serpent: "I will put enmity between you and the woman, and between your offspring and her offspring; he will bruise your head, and you will bruise his heel."[7]

Yes, here in the Book of Revelation chapter 12 time is running out for that primeval serpent deceiver. The time of his ultimate crushing is rapidly approaching, and his rage is turning into panic.

Chapter 13 brings us the two characters most likely to leap to mind when the subject of the end times arises. In fact, there have been enough nonsense Hollywood movies glorifying these two that even the unchurched man on the street associates them with the end of days.

Of course, I'm talking about the Beast—whose name is associated with the number 666—and his accomplice, the False Prophet. I am reluctant to invest much of your time or mine talking about this pair of failures. Furthermore, as I've stated more than once, speculation about the identity of the Antichrist/Beast or the solution to the 666 puzzle is pointless for blood-washed believers who are looking for Jesus's appearing. When the answers to those questions become evident, we won't be here to see them. I much prefer to talk about our wonderful Savior.

Nevertheless, let us briefly examine what God's Word says about them, if only to enjoy the reminder of how completely powerless they are when they finally come up against the unrestrained might of the Lord of Lords, the Captain of the hosts of heaven.

At the opening of the next chapter John witnesses the rise of the Antichrist:

> I stood on the sand of the sea. And I saw a beast rising out of the sea.... The dragon gave him his power and his throne and great authority. I saw one of his heads as if it was mortally wounded, but his deadly wound was healed, and the whole world marveled and followed the beast. They worshiped the dragon who gave authority to the beast. And they worshiped the beast, saying, "Who is like the beast? Who is able to wage war with him?" He was given a mouth speaking great things and blasphemies. And he was given authority to wage war for forty-two months.
>
> —REVELATION 13:1, 2–5

This is not a literal sea out of which John sees the Beast rising. As with the crystal sea before the throne of God, this is a sea of humanity. In other words, the Beast is not like one of the demonic creatures we have seen climb out of a bottomless pit. This is a human who emerges from the general population of earth.

According to John's description, blasphemous words seem to be his calling card. This suggests he will make claims that only the Savior of the world can legitimately make. This imposter is more than a "false Christ." He is an Antichrist. While presenting himself as the solution to all the world's problems, he personifies the opposite of everything the true Christ represents.

The passage quoted above says "the whole world...followed the beast." This is figurative rather than literal language. It indicates that many of earth's people fall for the Antichrist's deceptions. Yet the totality of John's vision makes it clear that a righteous remnant perseveres through the persecutions and pressures of the great tribulation.

Of course, there are two aspects of the Antichrist and his system that every man on the street can cite, even if he has never opened a Bible in his life. They are "the mark of the Beast" along with the number of his name, 666:

> He causes all, both small and great, both rich and poor, both free and slave, to receive a mark on their right hand or on their forehead, so that no one may buy or sell, except he who has the mark or the name of the beast or the number of his name. Here is a call for wisdom: Let him who has understanding calculate the number of the beast. It is the number of a man. His number is six hundred and sixty-six.
>
> —REVELATION 13:16–18

Oceans of ink have been spilled in feverish speculation, guesswork, deduction, and calculation concerning the "name" of the "man" whose "number" is 666. Countless candidates have been put forth over the centuries as clever, would-be code breakers found a variety of ways to squeeze the number 666 from the names of their favorite bad guys. Perhaps the most laughable of these theories I have personally encountered was circulating back in the eighties when, in all seriousness and earnestness, some of his political enemies noted that Ronald Wilson Reagan had six letters in each of his three names.

As I've stated repeatedly, guessing is pointless. This doomed character will remain hidden until well after the church is gone. What we can be certain of is that in the Beast system, individuals will not be able to legally operate in the world's economy without taking "the mark" of the Beast, whatever that may be.

What are we to make of this? Like with so many other mysteries of Revelation, we find illumination and understanding in a visit to the Book of Daniel.

Read the entirety of Revelation chapter 13, and you will discover that the Antichrist's accomplice, the False Prophet, sets up an idolatrous image of the Beast and commands everyone under the rule of the Beast system to worship that image. Those who refuse are condemned to suffer a horrible death.

Does this sound familiar to you? If you grew up in an evangelical church, you almost certainly heard a Bible story with elements very much like this as a child in Sunday school. For me this Old Testament event was depicted in riveting, nail-biting detail by Sister Gillicuddy with the help of her flannel graph. If you don't know what a *flannel graph* is, you're either under the age of fifty or weren't dragged to Sunday school at the age of six.

I am referring to "the three Hebrew children"—Shadrach, Meshach, and Abednego—cast into the fiery furnace by King Nebuchadnezzar. Let us briefly reacquaint ourselves with the account in Daniel 3 (sadly without the use of flannel cutout figures) and compare it to the events we see in Revelation 13:

> Nebuchadnezzar the king made an image of gold, whose height was sixty cubits and its width six cubits.... Then a herald cried aloud: "To you it is commanded, O peoples, nations, and languages, that at the time you hear the sound of the cornet, flute, harp, sackbut, psaltery, dulcimer, and all kinds of music, you should fall down and worship the golden image that Nebuchadnezzar the king has set up. And whoever does not fall down and worship shall the same hour be cast into the midst of a burning fiery furnace."
>
> —Daniel 3:1, 4–6

Note that six different types of instruments are listed in the passage above. That is six classes of instruments announcing mandatory worship of an image that is sixty cubits high and six cubits wide (three sixes).

Notice also that the command to worship the king's golden image applied to all "peoples, nations, and languages." This is a hell-inspired effort to establish a single world religion that serves as a forerunner of one to come in the distant future. Of course, you know the story. Three of Daniel's fellow exiles of Judah living in captivity in Babylon refused to violate their faith by worshipping Nebuchadnezzar's monstrosity. They were thrown into that furnace, yet God miraculously protected them.

The parallels to Revelation 13 are obvious and striking. It serves as an important reminder that the devil has no new tricks and no new agendas. His lust to be worshipped got him tossed out of heaven. He infected Adam and Eve with his "you shall be like God" deception. Here in Daniel chapter 3 he seeks worship through his proxy, Nebuchadnezzar. And centuries later he will run the same dictatorial scam through his puppet, Nero. It was Nero, foreshadowing the mark of the Beast, who required that all within the Roman Empire burn an incense offering recognizing the divinity of the emperor as a prerequisite to participating in Roman society and commerce. All these historic precedents were mere preludes and trial runs for the ultimate idolatrous deception that is coming after the catching away of the church.

There is another theme embedded in all these instances throughout history. Every time a deluded tyrant decides he is worthy of worship as a god, the true God preserves for Himself a righteous remnant who courageously refuse to bow their knees to the demonic pretender.

In Daniel's time a defiant Jewish remnant said, "Be it known to you, O king, that we will not serve your gods, nor worship the golden image which you have set up."[8] In the coming era of the Antichrist and his chief propagandist, the False Prophet, another Jewish remnant will take a similarly valiant stand.

Yes, during the forty-two months of the great tribulation the primary resistance to the rule of Antichrist will come not from evangelical sanctuaries, nor from Pentecostal "worship centers," nor from Catholic basilicas. The fiercest, most resilient opposition will come in totality from the Jewish synagogues.

It is the final verse of a very old song. And just as God miraculously delivered the remnant in Daniel, so shall He reward the faith and courage of the remnant during the great tribulation. God is going to show Himself strong for a very specific remnant of the nation of Israel during the tribulation period.

For most in our culture, including many Christians, the term *Antichrist* and the number 666 both tend to send a chill down the spine. Decades of Hollywood supernatural thrillers and horror movies have made sure of that. The typical "end of days" or demonic possession movie makes Satan look all-powerful and the people of God—usually portrayed in the form of a well-meaning but overmatched Catholic priest—hapless, helpless, and hopeless. This is hell-spawned propaganda.

I don't get the least bit nervous when I hear the number 666. In the same way the number seven typifies perfection and completeness in God's order of things, the number six represents incompletion and inadequacy. Put three sixes together, and you have inadequacy tripled, or perhaps cubed. Think of it as the numerical formula for "Can't do it. Never could. Never will." Referring to the Antichrist, the Bible says "the number of his name" is 666, but never forget that it symbolizes failure, futility, and defeat.

Yet, as I pointed out in chapter 7 concerning what to do if you miss the rapture, for those living through those night-marish days, the Beast and his mark will carry enormous implications for their daily lives. The Scriptures suggest that this "mark" will be a system of economic control that forces all who live under his demonic rule to accept it or be stripped of the ability to purchase anything—most importantly food. Food will be scarce and rationed, and its distribution controlled by the government during the great tribulation.

It is remarkable what people will do, or submit to, when they are profoundly hungry. In 2016 starving Venezuelans—a people whose economy was destroyed by the Marxist dictatorship of Hugo Chavez and his successor—broke into the Caracas zoo and killed several of the animals for food.[9] This drastic step came only after all the local grocery stores had been looted for what little food remained on shelves there.

A refugee from a developing nation once shared a piece of intriguing survival wisdom that vividly illustrates my point. He passed along a foolproof way to capture a whole herd of wild pigs.

He said all you have to do is begin regularly placing corn in an open field or forest clearing. Soon most of the wild pigs in the area will be partaking of the free corn. Free, easily accessible food is irresistible. After the pigs become habituated to the free meals, put up a single length of fence. The pigs will soon ignore the fence and continue coming for the food. Then add another length at a ninety-degree angle. The pigs will continue to come. Then add another length of fence.

Finally complete the pen by adding a fourth section, but include an open gate. The opportunity to eat free corn, upon which the pigs have now become dependent, will draw them right through the open gate. Then all you have to do is close the gate behind them. You now possess a completely helpless, dependent, captive herd of pigs. They will gradually and mindlessly sacrifice their freedom and self-sufficiency to fill their stomachs.

He who controls access to food controls the population. This truth lies at the heart of understanding the Antichrist's system and the mark of the Beast. Those who refuse the mark will find themselves locked out of a system that represents the only access to food. Accept the mark, and you get to eat, but you lose your eternal soul. Our Lord Jesus once asked, "For what does it profit a man if he gains the whole world and loses his own soul? Or what will a man give in exchange for his soul?"[10] During the great tribulation the answer is that millions upon millions will forfeit eternal life for a bowl of food. They will empty their souls for a chance to fill their stomachs.

In the final forty-two months of the tribulation period Satan's Antichrist enjoys a fleeting moment in history in which he holds the reins of power and experiences a measure of the worship he so desperately craves—but only because God allows him to do so. Well, *enjoys* is not the right word. As we have already seen, throughout this entire period calamities of unimaginable magnitude continuously spoil his coming-out party and damage his ability to maintain his hold on things. The devil's puppet is under assault and reeling from the very start.

Chapter 14 concludes the parenthetical interlude in which John gives us additional information before continuing the narrative about the judgment from heaven upon the activity of the Antichrist and his administration. In the fourteenth chapter we see in short order a prophetic glimpse of the final disposition of the 144,000, three angelic announcements to the earth, a blessing over those who keep the faith in spite of persecution, and a heavenly declaration of the manner in which the earth will be judged.

This last point deserves some additional attention.

> Another angel came out of the temple which is in heaven. He also had a sharp sickle. Yet another angel who had authority over fire came out from the altar. He cried with a loud voice to him who had the sharp sickle, saying, "Thrust in your sharp sickle and gather the clusters of the vine of the earth, for her grapes are fully ripe." The angel thrust his sickle into the earth and gathered the vintage of the earth, and threw it into the great winepress of the wrath of God.
>
> —REVELATION 14:17–19

The metaphor used here would have been well known to
everyone in John's day. The winepress was a common feature
on farms and estates in that part of the world, and grapes were
trodden to squeeze out the juice, sometimes referred to as the
"blood of the grape." In this case the angels are the reapers,
the vineyard is the earth, the grapes are the followers of the
Antichrist, the juice is blood, and the winepress is a certain
valley that is later identified as Armageddon.[11]

Who would tread the grapes? John later names Him Faithful
and True and declared, "He treads the winepress of the fury
and wrath of God the Almighty."[12] To this the prophet Isaiah
bore witness many years before, saying:

> "Who is this who comes from Edom with dyed garments
> from Bozrah? This one who is glorious in His apparel,
> traveling in the greatness of His strength?"
>
> "It is I who speak in righteousness, mighty to save."
>
> "Why is Your apparel red, and Your garments like him
> who treads in the wine vat?"
>
> "I have trodden the winepress alone."
>
> —ISAIAH 63:1–3

Parallel passages in Revelation and elsewhere testify of how
it all comes to a swift and decisive end for the Antichrist and
his vast army at the end of that brief season. They will believe
they are gathering in Israel's Valley of Megiddo to destroy
Israel and thereby secure control of the earth. In actuality they
are coming to be destroyed themselves once and for all time.

The Antichrist's final destruction is foreshadowed by yet
another series of catastrophes about to be poured out upon
his empire by a host of specially assigned angels. When John
departed from his timeline to include the parenthetical information of chapters 12 through 14, we saw the temple of God
opened in anticipation of an unprecedented series of events.
Now John returns to that same timeline, and he chronicles the

delivery of God's righteous judgment upon those who would, in folly and futility, continue to oppose God Almighty.

Chapter 15 records yet another worship service in heaven while the final judgments are made ready in the midst of a mighty display of God's glory. Chapter 16 tells of these seven judgments, in containers shaped like bowls, being released upon the throne of the Antichrist and the region of his domain.

- **The first bowl**—"The first went and poured out his bowl on the earth, and foul and grievous sores came on the men who had the mark of the beast and those who worshipped his image" (v. 2).

- **The second bowl**—"The second angel poured out his bowl on the sea. It became like the blood of a dead man, and every living creature in the sea died" (v. 3).

- **The third bowl**—"The third angel poured out his bowl on the rivers and springs of water, and they became blood" (v. 4).

- **The fourth bowl**—"The fourth angel poured out his bowl on the sun, and power was given to him to scorch men with fire" (v. 8).

- **The fifth bowl**—"The fifth angel poured out his bowl on the throne of the beast, and his kingdom was filled with darkness. They gnawed their tongues because of the anguish, and blasphemed the God of heaven because of their pains and their sores, and did not repent of their deeds" (vv. 10–11).

- **The sixth bowl**—"The sixth angel poured out his bowl on the great Euphrates River, and its water was dried up, to prepare the way for the kings from the East. Then I saw three unclean spirits like frogs coming out of the mouth of the dragon, out of the mouth of the beast, and out of the mouth of the false prophet. For they are spirits of demons, performing signs, who go out to the kings of the earth and of the whole world, to gather them to the battle of that great day of God Almighty" (vv. 12–14).

- **The seventh bowl**—"The seventh angel poured out his bowl into the air, and a loud voice came out of the temple of heaven, from the throne, saying, 'It is done!' And there were noises and thundering and lightning and a great earthquake, such a mighty and great earthquake, as had never occurred since men were on the earth.... Every island fled away, and the mountains were not found. Great hail, about the weight of a hundred pounds, fell from heaven upon man. Men blasphemed God because of the plague of the hail, because that plague was so severe" (vv. 17–18, 20–21).

The plagues that came upon Egypt were small compared with the magnitude of these disasters. Yet in spite of these judgments the Antichrist, blinded and borne along by an enmity beyond all reason, still does not relent in his maniacal obsession to attempt to search out and destroy all those on earth who put their trust in God.

Just as it seems the remnant of God's people on earth—overwhelmingly outnumbered by the forces of the Antichrist—are about to be utterly wiped out, the King rises from His heavenly throne as an excited murmur surges through heaven's hosts like a jolt of electricity.

The angels and the living creatures look on in wonder as the Prince of Glory strides to heaven's stables to release those eager chariot horses that haven't ridden the wind since they picked up the prophet Elijah. He slides a long, lean Galilean leg over a steaming white stallion that is snorting and pawing impatiently at the turf. Suddenly the crack of His long whip billows out like the crash of a thousand cannons. Behind Him an innumerable army of saints gives a thunderous battle cry and follows its captain back to the very spot from which He departed—Jerusalem's Mount of Olives.

As we are about to see, Jesus will return, just as He promised.

CHAPTER 10

The Return of the King

And Lord, haste the day when the faith shall be sight, the
clouds be rolled back as a scroll; the trump shall resound, and
the Lord shall descend, even so, it is well with my soul.[1]

—Horatio G. Spafford

His subjects call him "the Lionheart." King Richard I of England is beloved by his people, but he has been absent for years. No one is sure when he is coming back. Some are entertaining serious doubts as to whether he will ever return at all. Things seem to be falling apart in the king's long absence. What is worse, a devious usurper is now attempting to steal his throne.

Richard was born in Oxford in 1157. By the age of sixteen the tall, handsome prince had proved himself both fearless and skilled on the battlefield, earning the respect of his men, the admiration of the people, and a nickname.

In 1188, with his father, King Henry II, gravely ill, Richard Lionheart was further grieved at the arrival of news that Jerusalem and much of the rest of the Holy Land had fallen to the Muslim caliph, Saladin. Henry died a few months later, and Richard ascended to the throne of England. Yet the crown had scarcely come to rest upon his brow when he announced plans to lead a military expedition to recover Jerusalem from the forces of Saladin.

Before departing for Jerusalem with a large force, Richard

placed his domain under the administration of a trusted steward. Richard didn't know precisely how long he would be gone, although he knew his absence would be measured in years, not months. As he left, he made his people a solemn promise: "I will return."

Among those left behind was Richard's younger brother, John. Growing up in the shadow of his taller, more athletic, more popular sibling poisoned John's soul with the disfiguring toxins of resentment, jealousy, and envy. Not long after the king's departure for the Holy Land, John set plans in motion to put himself on his elder brother's throne.

It began merely as a whispering campaign, sowing doubts about the judgment and loyalty of Richard's designated administrator. In time the focus of the rumors, lies, and innuendos shifted to the king himself. Ultimately John organized a coup and deposed Richard's handpicked steward, who fled the country. This cleared the way for John to declare himself king of England. Eventually the distressing news of this insurrection reached the ears of Richard in the Holy Land. He was sorely tempted to return to England immediately and deal with his treacherous brother, but he and his men had come too far for too important an objective to simply turn around and go home. He knew they must first carry out the work they came to do. So he sent word back to the people of England: "Be patient. I am coming back soon. And when I arrive, I will set everything right."

A series of military victories followed quickly. Richard Lionheart's armies recaptured the strongholds of Acre and Jaffa in northern Israel, driving Saladin and his Islamic armies out of much of Israel. They then lay siege to Jerusalem herself. A desperate Saladin sued for peace and signed a treaty guaranteeing safe access to Jerusalem for Christian pilgrims and traders.

His mission largely accomplished, Richard began making his way back to England to deal with the outlaw usurper who had deceived so many. Once again he sent word home: "Do not lose heart. I am coming."

When Richard and his battle-hardened armies finally appear on the horizon, John and his coconspirators panic and flee. In February of 1194, five long years after his departure, Richard leads his armies back home and takes his rightful seat on the throne of England without a fight. The shameless insurrection evaporated like morning dew at the mere appearance of the true and rightful king.

As we have seen, for seven eventful years following the catching away of the church, a usurper—exploiting the physical absence of the rightful King of planet earth and His body, the church— will attempt to take a throne that does not belong to him. Satan, through his puppet the Antichrist, will spend the first three and a half years laying the groundwork. In the second half of that season he will actually position himself as a would-be ruler god, but with only partial success. All of this unfolds in Revelation chapters 4 through 16.

Chapters 17 and 18 are transitional. These chapters represent the indictment, conviction, and sentencing of this fallen, rebellious world system. In these chapters that system is personified as a harlot called Babylon the Great or "Mystery Babylon." This is the world system born of man's rebellion in the garden. The same spirit was on full display at the Tower of Babel in ancient Babylon. This self-glorifying religious system stands upon the hell-spawned lie that man can be self-sufficient and independent from his creator God. This is the original false religion.

Here, in two short chapters, we get a panoramic view of this age-old, millennia-long conspiracy to exalt man to the place of God, and we witness its defeat and ultimate demise.

It has never been, nor is it now, my purpose to try to positively identify every aspect of the details John gives in chapters

17 and 18. As I have stated before, those who are already blood-bought won't be present on the earth during these events. However, I will go so far as to say that chapter 17 chronicles the fall of a worldwide religious system. Let me hasten to add that I do not believe that this religious system is represented by anything that we currently see on the earth.

It seems as though the Antichrist uses this system for his own purposes during the first half of the tribulation but then comes to the point when he refuses to share the glory with anyone or anything other than himself. Those aligned with him help him overthrow the religious system then in place, paving the way for the Antichrist, or Beast, to declare himself as the only one worthy of worship.

The world's economic system is also disrupted and overthrown, symbolized by the destruction of the city of Babylon's system of commerce in chapter 18. I think it is instructive of how corrupt that system has become by the time it is destroyed, based on John's record of the kinds of transactions that take place in it: "The merchants of the earth will weep and mourn over her, for no one buys their merchandise any more: the merchandise of gold, silver, precious stones and pearls, fine linen, purple, silk and scarlet, all kinds of scented wood, all artifacts of ivory, all merchandise of costly wood, bronze, iron, and marble; and cinnamon and incense, myrrh and frankincense, wine, oil, fine flour and wheat, cattle and sheep, horses and chariots, and slaves and souls of men."[2]

Everything from gold, silver, and precious stones to slaves and the souls of men will be sold in the open marketplace when God's righteous judgment brings it all to a sudden and definitive conclusion.

The final four chapters of Revelation—chapters 19 through 22—reveal the glorious conclusion of God's plan to redeem fallen mankind and restore a curse-ravaged planet. We're about to witness the annihilation of a lie and of the "father of lies," who authored it.

A MARRIAGE SUPPER

Chapter 19 opens with a jubilant worship service in heaven hailing the victory of God's kingdom over the kingdoms of this fallen world. (See Revelation 11:15.) Have you noticed that every time we get a glimpse of heaven in John's vision, worship is taking place? That is no coincidence. God's heaven is a place of glorious, exuberant, exultant, lavish, never-ending worship. Now overlay that reality with the fact that our Lord exhorted us to pray, "Thy will be done on earth as in heaven." (See Matthew 6:10; Luke 11:2.) It becomes clear that the best way to prepare for a future eternity in heaven is to worship our God extravagantly today.

This victory celebration quickly transitions into a proclamation concerning another form of party, a wedding feast. John hears a thunderous voice announce:

> "Let us be glad and rejoice and give Him glory, for the marriage of the Lamb has come, and His wife has made herself ready. It was granted her to be arrayed in fine linen, clean and white." Fine linen is the righteous deeds of the saints. Then he said to me, "Write: Blessed are those who are invited to the marriage supper of the Lamb."
> —REVELATION 19:7–9

You will recall from our earlier exploration of first-century Jewish wedding customs that the wedding feast occurred only *after* the bridegroom and bride had been secluded away for seven days. Only after this week of intimate communion and bonding would the couple emerge to celebrate with family and friends. The verses above represent the announcement for that upcoming celebration. Jesus and His bride, the church, have been hidden away in heaven for a week of years as the tribulation period unfolded on earth.

At the angelic announcement of the upcoming wedding feast John falls down in awe and wonder at the feet of the messenger. This prompts a swift and emphatic correction from the angel:

> See that you not do that. I am your fellow servant, and of your brothers who hold the testimony of Jesus. Worship God! For the testimony of Jesus is the spirit of prophecy.
> —REVELATION 19:10

Please note that final sentence from the angel messenger. "The testimony of Jesus is the spirit of prophecy." Did you know that your testimony—that is, your personal redemption story— is a prophecy to the world concerning Jesus? Here in these last days shouldn't those of us who have been rescued from the domain of darkness and transferred to the kingdom of God's dear Son be telling about our relationship with our Savior to every person we meet? We should be shouting our stories from the mountaintops while time and opportunity remain. Our testimonies of Jesus are a prophetic word to this generation.

FAITHFUL AND TRUE

Following the jubilant announcement concerning the upcoming marriage supper John sees something truly extraordinary. Indeed, he witnesses the event for which all of creation has been longing and groaning since the fall of man:

> I saw heaven opened. And there was a white horse. He who sat on it is called Faithful and True, and in righteousness He judges and wages war. His eyes are like a flame of fire, and on His head are many crowns. He has a name written, that no one knows but He Himself. He is clothed with a robe dipped in blood. His name is called The Word of God.
> —REVELATION 19:11–13

There is no question about who this rider is. He is called "Faithful and True." If there has ever been a more appropriate description of Jesus, I've never heard it. Yet as if to remove all doubt, John adds that "His name is called The Word of God." This is the same John who, writing concerning Jesus in the first verse of the Gospel that bears his name, declared, "In the beginning was the Word, and the Word was with God, and the Word was God."[3]

The white horse rider we encountered back in chapter 6 was an imposter. But now we see the real deal, and there is no comparison. The sight of this rider is at once glorious and terrible to behold. Here the Savior appears not as a gentle, wounded Lamb but as a battle-ready King, armed and leading an innumerable host into conflict. As verse 14 reveals, "The armies in heaven, clothed in fine linen, white and clean, followed Him on white horses." Please note that just a few verses earlier in this chapter, in the passage concerning the marriage supper of the Lamb, we saw that the bride was adorned in "fine linen, clean and white."[4] Clearly the bride and this army are one and the same.

I will be among that brilliant linen-clad army. So will you if you truly know Him who is clothed with a "robe dipped in blood" and whose "name is called The Word of God." I have always wanted to stay as close to Him as I possibly can. I once told my congregation that when this moment in heavenly history arrives—when *Faithful and True* leaps upon that white charger to lead an army of saints to take possession of planet earth—do not be surprised if Jesus has to look over His shoulder and say, "Parsley, get on your own horse!" I just always want to be as close as I can to the One who died for me.

John's description of the Warrior King in His battle raiment continues:

> Out of His mouth proceeds a sharp sword, with which
> He may strike the nations. "He shall rule them with an

iron scepter." He treads the winepress of the fury and
wrath of God the Almighty. On His robe and on His
thigh He has a name written: KING OF KINGS AND
LORD OF LORDS.

—REVELATION 19:15–16

This is a Jesus that those who have spent their whole lives sitting under today's postmodern, feel-good preachers won't recognize. This warrior King with a sword in His mouth and fire
in His eyes is a far cry from the new-age, androgynous, group
therapy leader currently preached from many pulpits.

Yes, Jesus is the Prince of Peace, but before true peace can
return to earth, a war must be fought and won. An ancient
rebellion must be crushed like grapes in a winepress. A flood
tide of stored-up wrath, long held back by levees of grace and
patience, must be released upon the enemies of Christ.

Yes, our God is a God of love. Indeed, His is an immeasurable, relentless, furious love. Only a love as pure as this would
move a righteous, holy God to lay His only begotten upon an
altar of sacrifice so that a rebellious, thankless race of walking
dead men could know life again. Behold a love so intense that
it worked patiently for more than six millennia to bring history
to this very point—the ultimate quelling of an ancient, defiling,
misery-bringing rebellion. God's Word reveals that His nature
holds not only unfailing love but also a fierce anger against sin.
The principles of justice upon which He framed creation allow
no acquittal of the wicked outside the blood of an atoning
sacrifice.

As the preacher of Ecclesiastes wisely stated, there is "a time
for war and a time for peace."[5] On God's divine timetable this
is a time for war. It was John's privilege to prophetically glimpse
the Prince of heaven riding out against the Antichrist and the
multitudes who follow him. You and I will possess the privilege
of riding behind the true and rightful King.

A PROMISE FULFILLED

We began this journey at the Mount of Olives. There, on the crest of that rocky hill just east of Jerusalem, Jesus ascended into heaven. An angelic announcement accompanied His departure. "One day," the messenger promised, "He will return just as He has left."

Now, in John's Patmos vision, that day has come. He witnesses the fulfillment of that two-thousand-year-old promise. If we overlay John's vision with parallel prophecies in Ezekiel and Zechariah, a clear picture emerges of what this day will bring on earth.

An observer standing just outside the Old City of Jerusalem on that glorious day will see a brilliant flash of light in the sky. A portal will have opened between the heavenly dimension of the spirit and our material world. A patch of blinding white breaking through the clouds will ultimately come into focus. It is a Man in white on a white horse with an innumerable host of white-clad warriors behind Him. The lead rider, traveling at an incomprehensible speed, will be on a direct course to the Mount of Olives.

As the prophet Zechariah foresaw, the instant His feet touch that ancient piece of ground, a massive earthquake will rock the entire land as the Mount of Olives splits in half as if struck by God with a giant cleaver.[6] Half of the mountain will slide north as the other half slides south. Out of the rift valley that now separates the two halves will gush a torrent of water, long trapped in some subterranean chamber, flowing forth to create two new rivers in Israel. One goes west toward the Mediterranean Sea, and the other surges south through the Negev and into the Dead Sea.[7]

The Dead Sea has been "dead"—that is, devoid of life—throughout all of human memory because the Jordan River flows in but has no outlet. However, Ezekiel prophetically glimpsed this event and saw this new river turning the bitter waters of the Dead Sea sweet and hospitable to life once more.[8]

How accurate are God's prophets? Consider this. On one of my many trips to Israel I met with a Jewish community leader who showed me maps and charts derived from an extensive geological survey conducted by the government of Israel. He pointed to several dotted lines crisscrossing the territory of Israel. "Those lines," he told me, "are the locations of significant geological faults."

Then my host pointed to a particular spot on the map. "That is the Mount of Olives," he told me. "This fault runs right through the middle of it," he said, referring to one of the dotted lines. Then he added something that made the hair on the back of my neck stand up. "Oh, and it runs right through the Temple Mount as well." By the way, those same studies indicate the presence of a large body of freshwater buried deep beneath the subterranean rock of the Mount of Olives. Imagine that.

A sobering 2012 article in the *Jerusalem Post* examined the extreme likelihood that a significant earthquake will rock Israel or its vicinity in the near future. The report flatly stated, "Seismologists in Israel agree that a major earthquake is only a matter of time."[9] The same article quotes Ata Elias, an assistant professor of geology at the American University of Beirut, as saying:

> We know from historical records that at least twice in the last millennium along the entire fault line from the Red Sea up to Turkey were a major series of earthquakes in the 3rd to 6th century and then again between the 11th and 13th century.... Apparently the faults in the area have a cycle of 8–10 centuries, so we're due for another one.[10]

We can't know when the Mount of Olives will split in two, but we can know what literally earthshaking event triggers it.

It will happen when a pair of nail-scarred feet return to touch the last soil upon which they ever stood.

THE ARMY OF ANTICHRIST DESTROYED

The final three verses of chapter 19 describe the complete defeat of the Antichrist along with his sidekick, the False Prophet. Their immense force of deceived followers doesn't fare well either:

> Then I saw the beast and the kings of the earth with their armies gathered to wage war against Him who sat on the horse and against His army. But the beast was captured and with him the false prophet who worked signs in his presence, by which he deceived those who received the mark of the beast and those who worshipped his image. These two were thrown alive into the lake of fire that burns with brimstone. The remnant were slain with the sword which proceeded out of the mouth of Him who sat on the horse. And all the birds gorged themselves with their flesh.
>
> —REVELATION 19:19–21

This is the renowned "battle of Armageddon." It would be more accurate to call it the *slaughter* of Armageddon. According to an earlier glimpse of this battle revealed in chapter 14, the blood will flow as high as a horse's bridle for a length of one hundred and eighty-six miles.[11] Even so, the armies of Christ will suffer no casualties on this day. Revelation 19:21 tells us why: "The remnant were slain with the sword which proceeded out of the mouth of Him who sat on the horse." The method of destruction is a sword—not a physical sword, but one that comes out of Jesus's mouth. This means that a word is spoken by the King of Kings that causes the annihilation of an army of millions in an instant.

Zechariah 14:12 reveals additional detail: "And this will be the pestilence with which the LORD will strike all the peoples who go to battle against Jerusalem: Their flesh will rot as they stand on their feet, their eyes will rot in their sockets, and their tongues will rot in their mouths." No theatrical portrayal has ever approximated the horrifying reality of what that day will be like for the multitudes who follow the Antichrist.

In three short verses in Revelation 19, scarcely a footnote on John's long narrative, the Antichrist is utterly defeated, captured, and thrown headlong into the eternally unquenchable lake of fire.

That's right. On the day when Jesus's promise to return is finally fulfilled, it will all be over in less than an hour.

Then, from His vantage point on the freshly sundered Mount of Olives, our champion will look across the Kidron Valley and up to Jerusalem's eastern gate. Then perhaps the saints of God spontaneously begin prophesying to those gates by singing a portion of the twenty-fourth Psalm in unison:

> Lift up your heads, O you gates; and be lifted up, you everlasting doors, that the King of glory may enter. Who is this King of glory? The LORD strong and mighty, the LORD mighty in battle.
>
> —PSALM 24:7–8

As the redeemed of the Lord shout and sing, those gates will explode open. The Prince of heaven will go down through that valley, up the other side, through those ancient gates, and upward onto the Temple Mount. They called this hill Mount Moriah back when Abram proved his faith and obedience in his willingness to offer up his only son. The psalmist David and the prophets frequently referred to this very same stony prominence as Mount Zion.

Of course, there is another common name for this place. To the world's one-billion-plus Muslims, this is Al-Haram Al Sharif, "the noble sanctuary." As I write these words, the Al-Aqsa Mosque, the iconic Dome of the Rock, the Dome of the Chain, as well as four minarets dominate the crown of that ancient hill. These combine to make this spot the third-holiest piece of real estate in the Islamic world.

Nevertheless, it will not be the sight of that shiny golden dome that will be the focus of Messiah's attention as He crests that hill on that glorious day. A freshly built Jewish temple will be adorning that hill, shining white in the Judean sun. I do not profess to know how this will come to be. Frankly I don't care. I just know that God's Word declares it, and therefore you and I can count on it. At some point during the seven-year tribulation period, in association with the rise of the Antichrist, these Muslim shrines will either be moved or will have to share that elevation with what Israel's Jews expectantly call "the third temple."

On the day Jesus Christ returns to earth, He is going to sit down on the throne of His father David and begin an earthly rule of precisely one thousand years. What a season that will be. Next we will explore that ten-century reign of peace and what comes after it.

CHAPTER 11

The Reign of the King

Hebrew seers saw glimpses of the coming glory, heard notes of the coming harmonies. . . . They saw a Kingdom established over which a King should rule in righteousness and equity. As these men looked on they saw nature at peace, and in the midst of it a little child at play.[1]

—G. Campbell Morgan (1863–1945)

T HE MILLENNIUM. OUTSIDE its biblical context it is a term that simply denotes one thousand years. In context this word appears six times within the first seven verses of Revelation chapter 20. Perhaps God is trying to get our attention here.

In fact, John's narrative covers a thousand of the most remarkable years in all of human history in six short verses. He then jumps to the end of that period in verse seven.

The millennium is the unique pause in history's timeline in which King Jesus rules on an earth that is inhabited by both mortals and eternals. By that I mean there will be millions upon millions of survivors of the tribulation period who will still have earthly bodies that grow old and die. These are mortal men, women, and children. At the same time there will be untold millions of us who will have returned to earth with Christ and with glorified bodies that never age and never die.

There isn't a lot of detail in these six verses about those ten centuries of righteous government. Indeed, most of our understanding and insight into this glorious future period comes from other Scriptures, particularly from the prophetic pen of

Isaiah. He foresaw a golden age in which much of the curse that fell upon the earth at the fall of mankind in the garden has obviously been reversed. For example, in this era deadly, carnivorous animals no longer kill to survive:

> The wolf also shall dwell with the lamb, and the leopard shall lie down with the young goat, and the calf and the young lion and the fatling together; and a little child shall lead them. The cow and the bear shall graze; their young ones shall lie down together; and the lion shall eat straw like the ox. The nursing child shall play by the hole of the asp, and the weaned child shall put his hand in the viper's den. They shall not hurt or destroy in all My holy mountain.
>
> —ISAIAH 11:6–9

Isaiah also foresaw a day in which human life spans increase dramatically:

> There shall no longer be an infant *who lives only a few* days nor an old man who has not filled out his days. For the child shall die a hundred years old, but the sinner being a hundred years old shall be accursed...for as the days of a tree are the days of My people, and My chosen ones shall long enjoy the work of their hands.
>
> —ISAIAH 65:20, 22

In both passages Isaiah is describing a glorious glimpse of the millennium, Christ's one-thousand-year reign on earth. This will clearly be a wonderful time to be living on earth for two reasons. The primary and most obvious of these is that Jesus is in charge. Our wonderful Shepherd King will be physically present, ruling from Jerusalem. Again, Isaiah saw this:

> And the government shall be upon his shoulder. And his name shall be called Wonderful Counselor, Mighty God, Eternal Father, Prince of Peace. Of the increase of

his government and peace there shall be no end, upon the throne of David and over his kingdom, to order it and to establish it with justice and with righteousness, from now until forever.

—ISAIAH 9:6–7

This government will not be a democracy, a republic, or a parliamentary system. It will be a monarchy. Specifically it will be a theocratic monarchy, in which the Word of God serves as the constitution, and the Word made flesh as the sovereign ruler. Our King will be absolutely good and kind and just and benevolent. He will be filled with love for His subjects and have only their best interests at heart. In fact, He will have already laid down His life for them. What is even more amazing, according to Scripture, is that all of us who returned with Him in our new glorified bodies will be governing with Him!

A second and very much related reason this era is so remarkable is that for the first time in mankind's memory Satan will not be loose upon the earth to deceive, corrupt, and defile. To see why, let us back up and examine the opening verses of chapter 20:

And I saw an angel coming down out of heaven, having the key to the bottomless pit and a great chain in his hand. He seized the dragon, that ancient serpent, who is the Devil and Satan, and bound him for a thousand years. He cast him into the bottomless pit, and shut him up, and set a seal on him, that he should deceive the nations no more, until the thousand years were ended. After that he must be set free for a little while.

—REVELATION 20:1–3

What a wonderful passage of Scripture this is! I love the phrase "and shut him up." Of course, this means that an immense cover or lid of some sort will be placed over the opening of the bottomless pit. But it also means we won't be hearing from Satan for a very long time. This binding and imprisonment will force that lying, whispering, slandering, boasting loudmouth to literally *shut up*. I once preached this very point at one of our national conferences. The congregation shouted for ten minutes and refused to sit down. It is indeed a very happy thought.

This is the same ancient serpent who, on a Friday long past, tried to shut Jesus Christ up in a pit. It too had a massive lid rolled over it and a seal placed upon it. But that pit couldn't hold the Lord of Glory for even three days. The Dragon, on the other hand, stays sealed up until God, in His providence, briefly lets him out for a little season, and only because it serves God's purposes to do so.

THE FIRST RESURRECTION

Immediately after witnessing the business of binding and confining the serpent in the bottomless pit, John next sees "thrones," plural, and people sitting upon them:

> I saw thrones, and they sat on them, and the authority to judge was given to them.
> —REVELATION 20:4

Christ the King has just taken His place as the rightful and sovereign ruler of this world, and yet John sees not one throne, but many. Who might these be who have been granted "the authority to judge"? You and me, of course! These are the saints of God. Please recall that in 2 Timothy 2:12 Paul declares that "we shall also reign with Him." And in 1 Corinthians 6:3 he asks, "Do you not know that we shall judge angels?" Of course, the only angels in need of judgment are fallen ones. The Book of Jude reveals that the angels that participated in Lucifer's original rebellion have been "kept in everlasting chains under darkness for the judgment of the great day."[2]

This is that day, and it is indeed a "great" one. With their leader bound and gagged in a bottomless pit, a parade of disarmed, disgraced demonic spirits will be brought before God's people for judgment concerning all the wickedness, sorrow, sickness, hate, and violence they inspired through the centuries.

Remember the pleas of the quivering, sniveling pack of devils named "Legion" that Jesus ultimately cast into a herd of swine in Matthew chapter 8? While Jesus was still at a distance from them, they cried out, "What have we to do with You, Jesus, Son of God? Have You come here to torment us before the time?"[3] Two thousand years ago every demon in hell knew a time of judgment was coming for it. The millennium is that time, and you and I will be the instruments of that judgment.

A poignant scene quickly follows, in which John sees the "souls" of those believers who stood firm during the tribulation and were killed because they refused to worship the Beast or take his mark. These tribulation martyrs are actually resurrected before John's wondering eyes:

> They came to life and reigned with Christ for a thousand years. The rest of the dead did not come to life until the thousand years were ended. This is the first resurrection.
> —REVELATION 20:4–5

What did John mean by the term "the first resurrection"? Some people might find this confusing, but a careful reading of the Word reveals that, in reality, "the first resurrection" actually consists of a series of raptures and resurrections!

Stay with me here, and I believe you'll see what I mean. We already know about the rapture of the church. As we saw earlier, this is the catching away of the living saints along with the resurrection of the righteous dead, which occurs just prior to the seven-year tribulation period. This is the group you and I want to be sure we're in.

There is another rapture implied at the midpoint of the

tribulation period. In Revelation chapter 14 we see the 144,000 Jewish evangelists caught up to heaven.[4]

On the final day of the tribulation period, which also becomes the first day of the millennial reign, the mysterious "two witnesses" who vexed and frustrated the Antichrist experience both a resurrection and a rapture on the same day![5]

Before I move on, please allow me to note that these two witnesses preach for three and one-half years right under the Antichrist's nose in his Jerusalem base of operations. I frequently remind hostile members of the news media that, as this passage suggests, they are never going to be rid of preachers like me. We are always going to be here proclaiming truth and righteousness. You cannot kill us. If the poison pens of newspapermen and television pundits could have killed me, I would have been dead a thousand times over by now.

The same is true of God's two end-time preachers. They will preach for 1,260 days right under the Antichrist's headquarters window, and he will have to listen to them. At the end of that season God finally lifts His hands of protection and allows them to be killed. I don't believe there is any hint of hurt or defeat in this whatsoever, for to be absent from the body is to be present with the Lord (2 Cor. 5:8).

John foresees that for three days the bodies of the two preachers will lie in the streets of Jerusalem as the Antichrist throws a worldwide party. Think about that the next time you're watching the ball drop in Times Square as the whole wide world watches live via satellite. The Antichrist will have his television cameras and global news networks broadcasting the "defeat" of these two enemies of the Antichrist around the globe. "They're dead! They're finally dead," the news reporters will exult. The Antichrist's followers and sycophants will exchange gifts and throw jubilant parties in delirious celebration.

Then, three days later, according to your Bible, the blue cheeks of those preachers will flush rosy once more. With the whole planet looking on, their eyes will begin to blink, their limbs will begin to stir, and they will stand up. Upon standing they will begin to rise heavenward before the astonished eyes of a watching world.

Then later that day the martyred tribulation saints will be resurrected as well, in accordance with Revelation 20:4. Two verses later John makes an important editorial comment about all of this:

> Blessed and holy is he who takes part in the first resurrection. Over these the second death has no power, but they shall be priests of God and of Christ and shall reign with Him a thousand years.
>
> —Revelation 20:6

Please believe me when I say that you want to take part in that first resurrection! All of the resurrected righteous will be with Jesus in His glorious millennial reign and functioning as a royal priesthood throughout that thousand-year span of peace and glory.

As I mentioned previously, John's narrative jumps to the end of that period at verse 7 of chapter 20, moving quickly to the events that follow. Those events represent the closing chapter of the drama of human history and set the stage for a whole new adventure to begin.

THE END OF SATAN

As John reveals, the devil is briefly released from his subterranean cage at the end of that thousand-year period, and he, true to form, quickly seizes the opportunity to deceive all those willing to be deceived and to lead one last rebellion against God:

> When the thousand years are ended, Satan will be set free from his prison and will go out to deceive the nations which are in the four corners of the earth, Gog and

Magog, to gather them for battle. Their number is like
the sand of the sea. They traveled the breadth of the earth
and surrounded the camp of the saints and the beloved
city. But fire came down from God out of heaven and
devoured them.

—REVELATION 20:7–9

The obvious question here is, why? Why would God release
the devil after having him bound, silenced, and locked harm-
lessly away for a thousand years? The Word of God doesn't
answer that question explicitly, but it is not difficult to arrive at
an answer that harmonizes with biblical principles.

Keep in mind what I pointed out earlier about mortals
and eternals coexisting on the earth throughout this period.
Millions of individuals, enjoying long life spans and freedom
from calamities of nature, will marry and have children, grand-
children, great-grandchildren, and great-great-grandchildren
throughout this season of heaven on earth. Yet, while the reign
of King Jesus will roll back the curse on planet earth, it won't
remove mankind's God-given power to *choose*. God gifted
Adam and Eve with the power of choice, and every one of their
descendants has possessed and exercised the same power to
either accept or reject God's love and authority. This will be no
less true during Christ's millennial reign.

So, before God can bring the curtain down on this tired
old planet once and for all, those who have been born since
the beginning of the millennium will need an opportunity to
choose a side. Thus, the release of the devil provides one final
season of sifting to separate mankind's wheat from its chaff.

It's astonishing to contemplate, but as the Scripture above
foretells, millions upon millions—"like the sand of the sea"—
will follow after Satan in a foolish and futile attempt to unseat
King Jesus and His saints from the seat of authority in Jerusalem.
Even after having lived their whole lives in an earthly paradise
akin to the very Garden of Eden itself, they will fall for the

serpent's same old whispered lie: "You shall be like God." This is astonishing and a firm rebuke to all those who would dream of man being able to create a world without God.

Just as the deceived millions surround Jerusalem, fire from heaven falls and devours every last rebellious, idolatrous one of them. And as for Satan? The recompense that has been awaiting him since the day his narcissism and ambition first drove him mad and moved him to contemplate treason finally arrives:

> The devil, who deceived them, was cast into the lake of fire and brimstone where the beast and the false prophet were. They will be tormented day and night forever and ever.
> —REVELATION 20:10

Oh, what a moment that will be. What incalculable sorrow, grief, bloodshed, and misery that vile deceiver sowed in the earth. Now the father of lies has deceived his last victim. All that remains to be done before eternity can commence is some final accounting.

THE GREAT WHITE THRONE

Verse 11 of chapter 20 brings us a change of scene. John's vision shifts from the throne of Christ on earth to the courtroom throne of the Father in heaven:

> Then I saw a great white throne and Him who was seated on it. From His face the earth and the heavens fled away, and no place was found for them. And I saw the dead, small and great, standing before God. Books were opened. Then another book was opened, which is the Book of Life. The dead were judged according to their works as recorded in the books.
> —REVELATION 20:11–12

The end of this phase of mankind's history has come. It is time to attend to the bookkeeping. We have already observed several resurrections so far in John's narrative, but each of these had only involved the righteous dead. All of these come under the banner of "the first resurrection." Now the unrighteous dead—those who died rejecting God's gracious invitation to receive eternal life—are raised up as well. John says, "The sea gave up the dead who were in it, and Death and Hades delivered up the dead who were in them. And they were judged, each one by his works."[6]

This is the final resurrection, in which the wicked dead of all the ages are gathered to stand before God. All of the righteous have already been raised up and are now ruling and reigning with Christ. Now, in a single, convulsive instant, the earth gives up all of its remaining dead. The wicked belch forth from the bowels of the ocean depths, and hell empties itself of its human contents.

Unregenerate humanity stands before God to give an account of the deeds done in the flesh and to be judged by an infinitely just and holy God.

Back in chapter 6 we saw Death riding to and fro upon the earth as one of the four horsemen, with Hades as its companion. In the new era about to dawn, there will be no more death and therefore no need for a place to contain the spirits of the dead. Thus these two are cast into the eternal, unquenchable lake of fire right along with the eternal spirits of mankind's unrighteous billions:

> Then Death and Hades were cast into the lake of fire. This is the second death. Anyone whose name was not found written in the Book of Life was cast into the lake of fire.
>
> —REVELATION 20:14–15

In the very next chapter John will list eight categories of people who will be cast into the lake of fire:

> But the cowardly, the unbelieving, the abominable, the murderers, the sexually immoral, the sorcerers, the idolaters, and all liars shall have their portion in the lake which burns with fire and brimstone. This is the second death.
>
> —Revelation 21:8

The "cowardly"? Oh yes, the cowardly lead this list that includes murderers and sorcerers. The message here is that eternal torment awaits those too timid, too fearful of social disapproval, too terrified of displeasing all the wrong people to take a stand for Jesus in this life.

The "unbelieving"? Indeed. The skeptics, the doubters, the cynics, and the politically correct modernizers who in our era find the plain, hard truths of the Word of God too unpalatable and therefore refuse to believe them—these too will find themselves hurled headlong into this place called the lake of fire. Ironically the existence of such a place is precisely what many of these postmodern skeptics are most eager to deny.

THE REALITY OF HEAVEN AND HELL

Make no mistake about it; this lake of fire is a real place. This is no metaphor or allegory. The Hebrew word translated "lake" here, *linme*, is the very same one Luke used when referring to Lake Gennesaret in Luke 5:1. It is the same word Jesus used at the Sea of Galilee when He told His disciples, "Let us go over to the other side of the lake" in Luke 8:22. The lake of fire is a literal place of nonconsuming fire, unrelenting heat, and vicious turbulence.

I am aware this assertion has fallen out of fashion in some quarters of the Christian world. The two-thousand-year-old doctrine of a very real, absolutely eternal hell is one of a number of biblical teachings that a new generation of preachers and teachers find embarrassing or inconvenient in our postmodern world.

Of course, the heresy of universalism—the belief that all human souls ultimately end up in heaven, regardless of how they lived or what they believed in life—is an ancient one. As long as the church has had the revelation of the written Word of God, it has had a few who recoil at the horror of the implications of what it plainly says about hell. This, in spite of the red-letter words of John 3:36:

> He who believes in the Son has eternal life. He who does not believe the Son shall not see life, but the wrath of God remains on him.

In the New Testament we have two unimpeachable witnesses as to the reality of hell: the words of our Lord Jesus and those of His handpicked disciples.

Yes, like one of Israel's prophets of old warning the nation of impending judgment, the Savior warned His hearers frequently and forcefully of hell's reality. By some counts the Gospels contain seventy instances of our Lord talking about hell utilizing varying Greek and Hebrew terms and concepts familiar to His hearers. Seventy! Just one example is found in Matthew 13 when the Lord explains to the disciples His parable of the wheat and the tares:

> Therefore as the weeds are gathered and burned in the fire, so shall it be in the end of this world. The Son of Man shall send out His angels, and they shall gather out of His kingdom all things that offend, and those who do evil, and will throw them into a fiery furnace.[7]

Five chapters later we find another. In this case our Lord and Savior warns:

> Therefore if your hand or your foot causes you to sin, cut it off and throw it away. It is better for you to enter life lame or maimed than having two hands or two feet to be

thrown into eternal fire. And if your eye causes you to sin, pluck it out and throw it away. It is better for you to enter life with one eye than having two eyes to be thrown into the fire of hell.

—MATTHEW 18:8–9

In each of these cases and in dozens of others the Prince of Peace speaks plainly of hell as a literal place of literal fire and burning. Many of His warnings also depict this horrific locale as a place of darkness and of great suffering in both body and spirit, characterized by "weeping and gnashing of teeth."[8]

Contrary to some modern teachers who view hell as being only a temporary repository for the souls of unregenerate men and women, Jesus also clearly described it as being very much of *eternal* duration. In the parable of the sheep and the goats our Savior concludes the sobering illustration with a preview of the last words billions upon billions will ever hear as they stand before that Great White Throne:

Then He will say to those at the left hand, "Depart from Me, you cursed, into the eternal fire, prepared for the devil and his angels"...And they will go away into eternal punishment, but the righteous into eternal life.[9]

Please note that the Son of God uses the word "eternal" three times in the span of just two verses. Many modern theologians are quite happy to envision heaven as eternal but balk at acknowledging the same duration for hell. But you cannot keep your forever-and-ever heaven and jettison a forever-and-ever hell. Respect for the inerrant, infallible, immutable Word of God will not permit it.

The men the resurrected King of Kings sent into the world to proclaim the gospel also wrote of a coming time of fiery judgment and punishment. For example, the apostle Peter's second letter to the church brims with warnings to false teachers and heretics of coming judgment in hell. This rock-like member of the Savior's inner circle writes: "For if God did not spare the angels that sinned, but cast them down to hell and delivered them into chains of darkness to be kept for judgment...."[10]

Likewise, Jude's brief epistle warns sternly and vividly of the judgment and punishment that will one day befall the wicked and unrepentant. Like Peter's, his warning reveals that this punishment was originally intended for Lucifer and his fallen angel coconspirators:

> Likewise, the angels who did not keep to their first domain, but forsook their own dwelling, He has kept in everlasting chains under darkness for the judgment of the great day. Just as Sodom and Gomorrah, and the surrounding cities in like manner, gave themselves to immorality and went after different flesh, they serve as an example by suffering the punishment of eternal fire.[11]

This brings us back to John himself and his extraordinary glimpse behind the curtain of eternity recorded in the Book of Revelation. John's account made the reality of unending suffering a plain fact back in chapter 14, where he wrote:

> A third angel followed them, saying with a loud voice, "If anyone worships the beast and his image and receives his mark on his forehead or on his hand, he also shall drink of the wine of the wrath of God, which is poured out in full strength into the cup of His anger. He shall be tormented with fire and brimstone in the presence of the holy angels and in the presence of the Lamb. The smoke of their torment will ascend forever and ever. They have no rest day or night, who worship the beast and his image and whoever receives the mark of his name."
>
> —REVELATION 14:9–11

Hell will be as awful as heaven is wonderful. Both are very real and quite eternal. I am so unspeakably grateful the latter will be my everlasting home rather than the former. Please make sure I see you in heaven!

ALL THINGS BECOME NEW

We now enter the final two chapters of John's extraordinary vision. Chapter 21 brings us a new start for man and for creation. The old world, ravaged by the curse of sin, is defiled beyond reclamation. So the master Creator wipes the slate clean and starts afresh. In computer terms, God "reboots" the system:

> Then I saw "a new heaven and a new earth." For the first heaven and the first earth had passed away, and there was no more sea.
>
> —REVELATION 21:1

John's words point us back to the very first line of our Bibles: "In the beginning God created the heaven and the earth."[12] Now both of these have been re-created. These words are scarcely out of John's mouth when he sees the remade planet receiving an extraterrestrial visitor. "I, John, saw the Holy City, the New Jerusalem, coming down out of heaven from God, prepared as a bride adorned for her husband."[13]

Many believers have come to associate the term "New Jerusalem" with heaven, as if one were a euphemism for the other. But this is not heaven. The New Jerusalem comes *from* heaven *to* the earth. This great city is God's dwelling place in the material realm of earth. Just as the holy of holies in the tabernacle of Moses was God's dwelling place among His wandering people, so the New Jerusalem will be His habitation among men on earth for eternity. What a wonderful place this city is:

> And I heard a loud voice from heaven, saying, "Look! The tabernacle of God is with men, and He will dwell with them. They shall be His people, and God Himself will

be with them and be their God. 'God shall wipe away
all tears from their eyes. There shall be no more death.'
Neither shall there be any more sorrow nor crying nor
pain, for the former things have passed away."

—REVELATION 21:3–4

What beauty and wonder and glory this reborn world will
hold for the redeemed of God. We'll live in the paradise our
parents, Adam and Eve, forfeited. No curse. No sickness. No
pain. It is all so wonderful, even God is excited by it. He practically boasts to John: "Look! I am making all things new." [14]
Then God commands John to write the "faithful and true"
words the Father is about to pronounce:

He said to me, "It is done. I am the Alpha and the
Omega, the Beginning and the End. I will give of the
spring of the water of life to him who thirsts. He who
overcomes shall inherit all things, and I will be his God
and he shall be My son.

—REVELATION 21:6–7

It is done! This echoes Jesus's words on the cross. Indeed, the
work of redemption He legally secured through His sacrifice
has now been fully realized and made manifest. He who paid
a horrible price for the lifting of the curse has now seen it fully
and for all time repealed.

The balance of chapter 21 and the first five verses of chapter
22 make up a detailed description of the New Jerusalem. Then
twice in the final ten verses of this Bible book like no other
Jesus Himself makes a remarkable statement. It is a final invitation before the door is closed. In verse 7 He says:

Look, I am coming soon. Blessed is he who keeps the
words of the prophecy of this book.

Then again in verse 12:

> Look, I am coming soon! My reward is with Me to give
> to each one according to his work. I am the Alpha and
> the Omega, the Beginning and the End, the First and
> the Last.

Here among Revelation's final lines our wonderful Savior twice exhorts us to "look" for His soon coming. This compels me to ask: Are you looking? Are you anticipating His arrival to catch you away? Are you ready? I am. I have my bags packed, and I am ready to go! I am forgiven, washed in the blood, and I am expectantly, eagerly, enthusiastically looking for His appearing.

The Bridegroom is eager to return for His bride. He waits only for the Father to give the signal. The Holy Spirit and the bride—that is, the church—are eager as well:

> The Spirit and the bride say, "Come." Let him who hears
> say, "Come." Let him who is thirsty come. Let him who
> desires take the water of life freely.
>
> —REVELATION 22:17

I say it too. Come, Lord Jesus!

He *is* coming back, my friend. The first time He came as a baby wrapped in swaddling clothes while angels sang happy birthday and shepherds showed up to see if it was true. The second time He is coming as our conquering King, and no flesh will stand in His presence.

The first time He came as a suffering servant and gave His life a ransom for many. The second time He will come as a regent who will rule the nations with a rod of iron.

The first time He came in humility and scarcely raised His voice. The second time He is coming with a sword in His mouth—with the Word of authority that will become the absolute rule of the entire universe.

The first time He came, He suffered injustice and indignity, but the second time He comes, He will establish justice and restore the dignity of every man, woman, boy, and girl living under His gracious rule.

At His first appearing He was despised and utterly rejected of men. At His next appearing every knee will bow. Yes, the day is rapidly approaching in which every knee will bend—whether willingly or unwillingly—in awestruck recognition of who He truly is. Every tongue—even those that have damned Him, dismissed Him, derided Him, or denied Him—will openly declare that He alone is the only true and living God.

What a day that will be. And what unfathomable joys and adventures await those of us who will rule and reign with heaven's crown Prince. As the apostle Paul, citing the prophet Isaiah, declared, "Eye has not seen, nor ear heard, nor has it entered into the heart of man the things which God has prepared for those who love Him." [15] Yet Paul, living in the glorious dispensation of the Holy Spirit, hastens to add, "But God has revealed them to us by His Spirit." [16]

That selfsame Holy Spirit still speaks and reveals mysteries today. Those with an ear to hear—believers with hearts finely tuned to the frequency of heaven—hear a voice echoing through the hills of history and steadily rising in volume. That voice cries, "Get ready! Behold, the Bridegroom is coming!"

A Final Word

*Who is that coming up from the wilderness, like columns
of smoke, perfumed with myrrh and frankincense, with
all the fragrant powders of the merchant?*

*Look, it is [the King's carriage]! Around it are sixty mighty
men, the mighty men of Israel, all of them holding swords.*

—SONG OF SONGS 3:6–8

ABIGAIL PRETENDS NOT to hear the hurtful whispers of the
older women in the marketplace. From behind the veil that
declares she is betrothed and "off the market," she ignores their
stares. Custom and time-honored tradition demand that she
wear this veil until the day of the *nissuin*—that is, her "abduction" or carrying away to be with her beloved at last. She has
worn the veil in public for many weeks beyond the customary
one-year betrothal period. With each passing day she grows wea-
rier of well-meaning friends and relatives saying, "Any day now."

It has indeed been a very long time since her bridegroom
went away to prepare a place for them. Even some within her
own family have begun to wonder out loud whether he is ever
returning at all. Now each new day becomes a burden instead
of a delight. She loves her family, and she knows they love
her, but she has been promised something that none of them
can provide. She longs for more—and her bridegroom said he
would give it to her. She is ready to begin the future she had
anticipated for so long. *When?*

Disappointment and discouragement assail her. At times she
is tempted to give in to the voices of doubt that surround her.

During the day she can keep her mind occupied by helping her mother with the unending yet familiar tasks that come with managing a household. But at night, when the house is quiet, her mind wanders into unsafe territory.

Unbidden thoughts come to her faster than arrows could fly. "You're not so special. He's forgotten about you. He doesn't really care. You'll always be alone. No husband, no children, no future. Desolate and despised. Ignored and humiliated. Aged and infirm. Threadbare and penniless. Heartbroken and…"

Avigail gasps and sits up in bed. She cannot allow herself to think that way! She remembers her betrothed's voice, his touch, the look in his eyes as he said good-bye to her more than a year ago. She thinks of all the gifts he has sent her as pledges of his devotion. He said he would come back for her. She believed his words then, and she believes them still. In her heart she is sure that he is faithful and true. She will not be moved. Soon enough the mockers and skeptics will see that she was right to put her faith in him. He will fulfill his promise to her—and she will continue to trust him, no matter how long she has to believe.

So she waits. She watches. She both longs for and cherishes the thought of his appearing.

It is late—sometime around midnight—and the entire household is asleep, save Avigail. She has arisen quietly to attend to the clay pot lamp in the window, replacing with a fresh lamp the one now growing low on oil. This has been her nightly practice for a very long time now. Her father routinely grumbles halfheartedly about the mounting cost of so much oil, but she pays him no mind.

Suddenly the distant yet unmistakable sound of a ram's horn *shofar* cuts through the thick night air and echoes through the valley. Avigail freezes, wondering if she is dreaming. No. There it is again. A little louder this time! It is followed by the distant sound of a shouted chant:

The bridegroom cometh! The bridegroom cometh!

Avigail's heart thrills. It's him! He's come for me!

She runs through the house shouting, and dashes to her room to quickly dress. The things she had packed months ago are still sitting by her door. The white linen wedding garments she had so carefully sewn and kept unsoiled are among the belongings ready to be carried away by the wedding party. A few minutes more, and she hears a knock at the door.

He stands at her threshold! It is all true! He has come for her, just as he promised! Avigail feels as though she will burst with the flood of emotions that overtake her. There is a flurry of activity, including a tearful goodbye to her family, and she is on her way to her new home.

She scarcely notices the journey. He is near, and that is all that matters. He is more wonderful than she dared to dream. And for the rest of her life she will be the focus of his loving attention.

Arriving in her new home almost overwhelms Avigail's senses. It is more opulent and extravagant than she could have possibly imagined. The colors are brighter and more vivid than any she had previously experienced—almost as if she had lived her whole former life in a world of shades of gray. The trees, flowers, and grasses seem to shimmer and glow as if illuminated from within. The plants in his garden are extraordinary: roses, iris, narcissi, rue, oleander, lavender, myrrh, balsam, citron, orchids, mint, spikenard, marjoram, hyssop, thyme, and so many more. Every breeze brings a fresh new fragrance to delight her.

The sounds of this new domain are beyond description, especially the music. Avigail hears melodies and harmonies she hasn't known were possible. Even the wind in the trees and the babbling of the crystal-clear fountains seem to join in every song.

Every new discovery brings Avigail a fresh thrill of wonder. But the joys of the bridegroom's estate pale in comparison to the experience of being in the presence of the bridegroom himself.

He holds her close and looks into her eyes. "I did this for you," he says, and she knows in her heart it is true. Even so, she can scarcely believe that she is the object of such abundant affection and the recipient of such lavish grace.

He is beyond wonderful in every aspect—good, kind, loving, caring, compassionate, thoughtful, intelligent, witty, wise— and respected, influential, and powerful. Being by his side and knowing that they will be together forever brings complete peace to Avigail and fills her with confidence and contentment.

So this is what it is like to be loved by someone so supremely that no price is too high, no sacrifice too great, no obstacle too insurmountable to keep them apart. She will always be grateful to God for bringing her to the bridegroom's attention.

Here, in this place of beauty and splendor, Avigail finds the true purpose for which she was formed by a wise and wonderful Creator. It doesn't really matter what she will be asked to do as long as she can stand by her bridegroom and give him all her heart, overflowing with fearless love and relentless devotion. This is true peace. This is real rest. This is joy unspeakable and full of glory. It all began in a moment, but it would never come to an end.

He is coming back, just as He said. This is a truth more constant than the sunrise. The faith of those who are waiting for His appearing will be vindicated as He splits the eastern sky, heralded by a heavenly trumpet and accompanied by a shout of triumph. He has gone to prepare a place for us, and He will come again and receive us to Himself. He is Faithful and

True. His promises are unbreakable, and His commitments are unshakable. And we—all those who confess Him as Savior—will find eternity in His presence filled with every benefit it is God's pleasure to bestow upon us, the objects of His eternal affection. The glory of the day of the Bridegroom's return will surpass our best day on earth more than the glory of the sun surpasses that of the moon.

May every heart that is lifted up in anticipation of His coming give its affirmation to what John wrote so long ago: "He who testifies to these things says, 'Surely I am coming soon.' Amen. Even so, come Lord Jesus!"[1]

Afterword

I HAVE BEEN EXTREMELY blessed and honored to have studied and taught on the return of Christ for a large sum of my life, and I have shared in many great debates on the topic. This book has been a breath of fresh air. *The Finale* leaves the heart stirred with so much more than something final—with a strong desire for things eternal. I have been left with a greater anticipation for the return of Christ, to see our Bridegroom come back in all of His glory. Oh, that the whole world would know that we are His and He is ours! What a glorious covenant and commission to tend to as we watch and pray!

This beautifully written piece of literature not only stokes the fire of love for Jesus but also challenges the mind to deeper knowledge of God's Word regarding Christ's return. Pastor Parsley has carefully taken time to explain difficult topics that have been a source of debate throughout history, and he has brought refreshing clarity to both heart and mind.

My prayer for you is that this has not just been another book that you will have read and replaced to your shelf but that every word will continue to resonate in your spirit and remind you of the precious relationship and covenant we have with Christ, our Bridegroom. Without a doubt, He is coming back for His Bride! He *will* return for a church without spot or blemish, and what a day that will be! This is His promise to us, and He is always faithful to complete every promise, above and beyond, every single time. Let us not be caught unaware or surprised, let us be about our Father's business, and let us ever be diligent to share the unwavering gospel of Jesus.

—DR. PERRY STONE
PERRY STONE MINISTRIES
VOICE OF EVANGELISM/OMEGA CENTER INTERNATIONAL

Notes

Prologue

1. See Ephesians 5:32.

Chapter 1 | The Promise

1. "Second Coming of Christ-Quotations & Illustrations," Precept Austin, updated September 17, 2016, accessed November 14, 2016, www.preceptaustin.org/second_coming_of_christ.

2. Alexander P. Forbes, *A Short Explanation of the Nicene Creed* (London: Oxford, 1852), 8–9.

3. James A. Kleist, *The Didache, The Epistle of Barnabas: The Epistles and The Martyrdom of St. Polycarp, The Fragments of Papias, The Epistle to Diognetus* (New York: Paulest Press, 1948), 24.

4. J. H. Parker, *The Epistles of S. Cyprian With the Council of Carthage on the Baptism of Heretics*, vol. 17 (Boston: Harvard University, 1844), 147.

5. Karl Hess, "Prayer for the Speedy Return of Christ to Judgment," De Profundis Clamavi ad Te, Domine, October 29, 2015, accessed November 14, 2016, https://deprofundisclamaviadte domine.wordpress.com/2015/10/29/prayer-for-the-speedy-return-of -christ-to-judgment-luther/.

6. Reginald Stackhouse, *The End of the World?: A New Look at an Old Belief* (Mahwah, New Jersey: Paulist Press, 1997), 47–49.

7. Jonathan Edwards, "The Final Judgment," Biblebb.com, accessed November 14, 2016, http://www.biblebb.com/files/edwards /final-judgment.htm.

8. Billy Graham, "Answers—July 17, 2014," Billy Graham Evangelistic Association, accessed November 15, 2016, http:// billygraham.org/answer/christs-second-coming-will-be-glorious-for -all-to-see/.

9. Calvin penned a commentary for every New Testament book except one—the final Book of our Bibles—Revelation.

10. Bob Utley, "Views of the Second Coming," ibiblio.org, accessed November 15, 2016, http://www.ibiblio.org/freebible commentary/pdf/EN/second_coming_theories.pdf.

11. See 1 Chronicles 12:32.

12. See Acts 1:11.

CHAPTER 2 | UNTANGLING THE TIMELINE

1. *The Book of Revelation as Illustrative of the History of Religion* (Newcastle, Great Britain: Whittaker & Co., 1841), 35–36.

2. "9/11: Timeline of Events," A&E Television Networks, LLC, accessed December 22, 2016, http://www.history.com/topics/9-11 -timeline; "Timeline for the Day of the September 11 Attacks," Wikipedia, accessed December 22, 2016, https://en.wikipedia.org /wiki/Timeline_for_the_day_of_the_September_11_attacks; Lawrence Wright, *The Looming Tower* (New York: Knof Doubleday Publishing Group, 2006).

3. See Matthew 28:20.

4. See 1 John 2:18.

5. See 2 Thessalonians 2:3.

6. See 2 Thessalonians 2:8.

7. See Daniel 7:8.

8. See Daniel 9:26.

9. See Jeremiah 30:7.

10. *The Dark Knight*, directed by Christopher Nolan (2008; Burbank, CA: Warner Home Video, 2008).

11. See Revelation 1:3.

12. F. W. Farrar, *The Early Days of Christianity* (New York: John W. Lovell Co., 1882), 470.

13. See Matthew 24:2; Mark 13:2.

14. An abundance of early Church tradition attests that John based his ministry in Ephesus and built Mary, the mother of Jesus, a house there in accordance with the Lord Jesus's directive from the cross that the beloved disciple care for her. Today tours of the ruins of Ephesus include a stop at an archaeological site credibly believed to be that house. (See Clinton E. Arnold, ed., *Zondervan Illustrated Bible Backgrounds Commentary: Hebrews to Revelation* [Grand Rapids, MI: Zondervan, 2002]).

Chapter 3 | Jesus Revealed

1. G. Campbell Morgan, *Exposition of the Whole Bible* (Eugene, OR: Wipf and Stock Publishers, 2010), 533.

2. See Revelation 1:10.

3. See Revelation 1:1.

4. See Matthew 17:2–3.

5. See Revelation 1:3.

6. See Revelation 1:9–11.

7. See Revelation 1:17–18.

8. See 2 Timothy 3:16–17.

9. See Revelation 3:22.

10. See Colossians 3:2.

11. See Ephesians 5:27.

12. "Holy, Holy, Holy," by Reginald Heber. Public domain.

Chapter 4 | Dry Bones Live Again

1. Dennis M. Swanson, "Charles H. Spurgeon and the Nation of Israel," accessed November 21, 2016, http://www.spurgeon.org /misc/eschat2.htm#note48.

2. "Programme and External Relations Commission (PX) Occupied Palestine," United Nations Educational, Scientific, and Cultural Organization, April 11, 2016, accessed November 21, 2016, http://unesdoc.unesco.org/images/0024/002443/244378e.pdf.

3. "PM Slams UNESCO Resolution Ignoring Jewish Connection to Temple Mount," *Times of Israel*, accessed April 16, 2016, http://www.timesofisrael.com/pm-slams-unesco-resolution-ignoring -jewish-connection-to-temple-mount/.

4. Many translations render the Greek word here, *aetos*, as "vultures."

5. Charles H. Spurgeon, "The Church of Christ (1855)," Blue Letter Bible, accessed November 21, 2016, https://www.blueletter bible.org/Comm/spurgeon_charles/sermons/0028.cfm, emphasis added.

6. See Matthew 24:2; Luke 21:6.

7. See Ezekiel 37:2.

8. See Ezekiel 37:3.

9. See Matthew 24:35; Mark 13:31; Luke 21:33.

10. See Matthew 24:6, 8.

CHAPTER 5 | LABOR PANGS AND THE GREAT TRANSITION

1. Martin Luther, *Luther's Correspondence and Other Contemporary Letters*, vol. 2 trans. and eds. Preserved Smith and Charles M. Jacobs (Philadelphia: Lutheran Publication Society, 1918), 881.

2. "The Cohen / DNA Connection," Judaism Online, accessed November 22, 2016, http://www.simpletoremember.com/articles/a /cohanim-dna-connection/.

3. See Numbers 19:1–10.

4. See 1 Thessalonians 5:9.

5. See Matthew 23:38–39.

CHAPTER 6 | RAPTURE READY

1. As quoted in Spiros Zodhiates, *The Behavior of Belief* (Grand Rapids, MI: Eerdmans, 1959), 87.

2. See 1 Thessalonians 4:17.

3. See 2 Corinthians 6:14–15, NKJV.

4. James Strong, *The Exhaustive Concordance of the Bible* (Boston: Hunt & Eaton, 1890).

5. See 1 Thessalonians 4:17, emphasis added.

CHAPTER 7 | HOW TO CATCH UP AFTER
THE CHURCH HAS BEEN CAUGHT UP

1. Vance Havner, "Quotes Related to the Return of the Lord," Precept Austin, 2014, accessed November 22, 2016, http://precept austin.org/second_coming_of_christ.htm.

2. Richard Pallardy, "Haiti earthquake of 2010," Encyclopædia Britannica, last updated August 18, 2016, accessed November 22, 2016, https://www.britannica.com/event/Haiti-earthquake-of-2010.

3. See Romans 10:13, KJV.

4. "There Is a Fountain Filled With Blood" by William Cowper, Cyberhymnal.org, accessed November 22, 2016, http://www .cyberhymnal.org/htm/t/f/tfountfb.htm.

5. See 2 Thessalonians 2:11.

6. See Matthew 24:44.

CHAPTER 8 | THE LION-LAMB OF GOD

1. Matthew Henry, *An Exposition of the Old and New Testament* (London: Joseph Robinson, 1839), 661.

2. See Revelation 5:2.

3. See Revelation 5:5.

4. See Revelation 5:6.

5. See Revelation 6:14.

6. See Joel 2:10.

7. See Revelation 14:4–5.

CHAPTER 9 | DECODING THE ANTICHRIST

1. J. Dwight Pentecost, *Things to Come: A Study in Biblical Eschatology* (Grand Rapids, MI: Zondervan, 2010), 235.

2. See Revelation 8:13.

3. See Revelation 9:12.

4. J. H. Jowett, *The Epistles of St. Peter* (Grand Rapids, MI: Kregel Publications, 1993), 54.

5. See Revelation 11:15.

6. See Genesis 12:3, paraphrased.

7. See Genesis 3:15.

8. See Daniel 3:18.

9. Harriet Alexander, "Hungry Venezuelans Break Into Caracas Zoo and Butcher a Horse," Telegraph Media Group Limited, August 19, 2016, accessed November 23, 2016, http://www.telegraph.co.uk/news/2016/08/19/hungry-venezuelans-break-into-caracas-zoo-and-butcher-a-horse/.

10. See Mark 8:36–37.

11. See Revelation 16:16.

12. See Revelation 19:15.

CHAPTER 10 | THE RETURN OF THE KING

1. "It Is Well With My Soul" by Horatio G. Spafford. Public domain.

2. See Revelation 18:11–13.

3. See John 1:1.

4. See Revelation 19:8.

5. See Ecclesiastes 3:8, NIV.

6. See Zechariah 14:4.

7. See Zechariah 14:8.

8. See Ezekiel 47:8.

9. Linda Gradstein, "Expert: 'When" Not "If" Large Mid-East Quake Due." *Jerusalem Post*, July 16, 2012, accessed January 5, 2017, http://www.jpost.com/Features/In-Thespotlight/Expert-When-not -if-large-Mid-East-quake-due.

10. Ibid.

11. See Revelation 14:17–20.

CHAPTER 11 | THE REIGN OF THE KING

1. G. Campbell Morgan, *The Westminster Pulpit vol. I: The Preaching of G. Campbell Morgan* (Eugene, OR: Wipf and Stock Publishers, 2012), 257.

2. See Jude 6.

3. See Matthew 8:29.

4. See Revelation 14:1–15.

5. See Revelation 11:11–12.

6. See Revelation 20:13.

7. See Matthew 13:40–42.

8. See Matthew 8:12; 13:42; 22:13; 24:51; Luke 13:28.

9. See Matthew 25:41, 46.

10. See 2 Peter 2:4.

11. See Jude 6–7.

12. See Genesis 1:1.

13. See Revelation 21:2.

14. See Revelation 21:5.

15. See 1 Corinthians 2:9.

16. See 1 Corinthians 2:10.

A FINAL WORD

1. See Revelation 22:20.